How Much Do You Know About Derek?

His famous home run: Derek hit a homer in Game 1 of the 1996 American League Championship Series

His favorite sport other than baseball: Basketball

His favorite athlete: Michael Jordan

His favorite athlete from childhood: Dave Winfield

His favorite food: Chicken parmesan

His favorite place to visit: Puerto Rico

Look Inside for More Fabulous Facts About Derek!

Derek Jeter

Pride of the Yankees

An Unauthorized Biography

Patrick Giles

St. Martin's Paperbacks

DEREK JETER: PRIDE OF THE YANKEES

ISBN: 0-312-97110-9

Printed in the United States of America

St. Martin's Paperbacks edition / April 1999

10 9 8 7 6 5 4 3 2

To my brother

Acknowledgments

*Fanaticism? No. Writing is exciting
and baseball is like writing.
You can never tell with either
how it will go
or what you will do . . .*
*——Marianne Moore,
"Baseball and Writing"*

Baseball and writing are alike in another way—both are team efforts. The home run may be Derek Jeter's, but the playing of a long line of fellow Yankees, by deed and example, helped make that winning swing possible. So it is with any book. I have a lot of people to thank for helping me get to bat, teaching me how to swing and how best to run, and how (hopefully) to cross home plate.

I have to thank everyone who spoke to me, and provided crucial insights into Derek Jeter's remarkable career and extraordinary fame. All of them were willing to talk (if not always for attribution); all were also concerned the book they were contributing to would be fair to its subject. I hope none of them are disappointed.

My agents, Jane Dystel and Miriam Goderich, and their plucky assistants, brought their skill and considerable energies to the project. It was Miriam's passion for the Yankees that led me to the story of one of them. At

St. Martin's Press, Associate Editor Glenda Howard has been a pleasure to work with. Thanks also to Associate Publisher John Rounds and Mass Market Publisher Matthew Shear.

If Derek Jeter embodies what is best in a baseball player, my sports researcher, Mike McCue, director of the Teaneck, New Jersey Public Library, provides a blueprint of what a baseball lover should be: someone who savors and remembers every moment of the game, and communicates that devotion effectively. Working with him was one of the real pleasures of this journey.

Scott Melvin literally gave me the space to be a writer, and Glenn Campbell the ability to use all the spaces I need to be one. Michael Cunningham convinced me I *was* a writer, whether I liked it or not, and Arthur Schwerdt and Sr. Mary Donald, RSM, taught me how to read and, thus, want to *become* a writer. And nobody in New York can either dream of or do writing without the support of the New York Public Library and its staff. Dena Santoro, Otto Coca, Robert White, Thomas Savage, Bruce Patterson and Phillip Fried, William Walker, Patrick Merla, Ernesto Mestre, Nancy Lemann, Bob Rideout, Richard Wheeler, Michael Corbett, Samuel J. Rosenblum, and Alex Fischer all provided crucial support. Calvin Giles tolerated the intrusion of Yankee books, clippings, and videos into our lives, and Margaret Giles Kerlin and her daughter, Kaitlyn, didn't let distance get in the way of enthusiasm.

The Kalamazoo Public Library is packed with valuable information on Derek Jeter's early baseball days, and its staff are diehard Jeter fans. Thanks to Saul Amdursky, director of the library; and staff members of the Adult Services Department, Local History/Community Information, including Margean Gladysz, Community Information librarian; Library Aides Kris Rzepczynski and Kristian O'Hare; and Library Assistant Joni Mc-

Donald. Without their efforts, a vital segment of the player's life story couldn't have been included in this book.

Thanks to John Berger, Jonathan Green of Globe Photos, and Tim Broekema of the *Kalamazoo Gazette* for allowing me to reproduce photographs, and Andrew Boorstyn of *Interview* for time off to work.

Sports journalism is an underrated genre. Studying the life of Derek Jeter allowed me to sample fine writers I might never have discovered, and to spend more time with some I already admired. This book wouldn't be possible without the beat work and reports done by several champs (a breakdown of authors and publications appears in the Bibliography).

Thanking them leads me to extend final gratitude to a colleague of theirs. I learned to read (in part) via the sports books my brother, Mark Hudson Giles, brought home from the library when we were kids. I still remember fragments of *The Pee Wee Reese Story*, *The Mel Ott Story*, and *The Baseball Encyclopedia*, among others. Through his example, reading and writing became, for me, as essential as water or breathing or light. In several essential ways, my growth as a person and a writer were both made possible by him, as well as the support of his wife, Diane Kelley Giles, and the amazing Matthew Hudson and Robert Bruce Giles. One of my biggest hopes is that this book can at least approach those sports books we both read and learned from—and inspire other readers to put the book down and join the game.

Patrick Giles
30 November 1998
New York, New York

Contents

At the Palace of Baseball

For starters: Derek Jeter always wanted to and now plays in what he considers the number-one baseball stadium in the world. The choice displays his unerring preference for the best, one he seems to have had even before he began to play baseball. The 75-year-old Yankee Stadium will always be the most beloved place in which to play.

If you follow this sport (or just Derek Jeter), there is probably no more awesome a sight than the gray diamond of Yankee Stadium afloat with illumination on the edge of the Bronx on a cool mid-October night. The burning field lights, the enormous murmur of fifty-seven thousand fans hanging on every moment inside, the hundreds of people stirring eagerly outside including fans and police and reporters, the light sting of autumn air, all mean one thing: It's a World Series Game, an event that has happened here more than in any other place in the world, and not just any World Series but a *Yankee* World Series. But even though it's only the latest attempt to up the number of World Series titles won by this club from 23 to 24, the city has been hopping with excitement as if the title's never been won before.

On this night in October 1998, the air seems to literally crackle with collective tension, a tension that's been building like a storm all year, for there has never been a season like this one. The New York Yankees were pegged to take their place representing the American League in the World Series from the season's beginning. And they've obliged the sports fortune tellers by winning 114 games and bringing their fans (who are not just local but national, even worldwide) into the stadium in record numbers. For weeks, New Yorkers had been barely able to control their excitement as their team took the Eastern Division handily from the Texas Rangers; then, after a few false steps, rallied and clobbered the Cleveland Indians in a clinching game that left thousands of New Yorkers too exhausted from triumph to go to sleep when it was over.

Now, this Saturday night, Game 1 of the World Series is in full swing. Outside the stadium, near the players' entrance, several teenage girls (some with parents in tow) and a cluster of young women are already patiently waiting in an informal stakeout. One glance, and you don't even have to ask who their target is. His player's number is on the Yankee jerseys they've just bought, or inked onto the baseball hats they're wearing. His face beams from photos that the girls have clutched in ready hands, in hopes of having them autographed, and on baseball cards collected over several years. And his name is on their lips, but whispered, in anticipation, as if they are saving their voices.

After the game, the instant he appears, the whispers explode into a roar.

"DEEERRRREEEKKKKK!" a young woman who had been quiet and unassuming a moment earlier bellows, her whole body fueling the shout. Two preteens in front of her jump up and down like human pom-poms, hair flying and arms waving. The mother guarding them seems a little less excited, but she too calls his name and, if you step back a few paces, you can hear it sailing across this Bronx intersection late at night:

"Derek! Derek! I love you! Derek . . . ?"

But you wouldn't step back. You'd be as caught up in the sudden fervor as everyone else, pressing forward, face cracking open in a huge smile without even realizing it, eager to get as close as you can to "*The* Man at Home Plate," as one of his young admirers put it during an exultant seventh inning, the young baseball star who has captivated fans of all kinds since he first stepped up to bat four seasons ago, the hope of the game's future and the man we're already calling the Pride of the Yankees. . . .

First Inning

The Idol

"Is that him? Derek! It IS? DEREK! Derek?..."

What's amazing when you first actually see Derek Jeter is how well he handles all of this—the attention, the idolatry, the scrutiny.

He returns every smile and passes with a strong but casual walk. In the low night lights, he seems less the earnest young man seen earlier running, jumping, and throwing with such grace under dazzling stadium lights; the dark makes him look a bit older, more romantic. This is perfect for the crowd facing him now. They love baseball, but they LOVE Derek Jeter.

He gets more fan letters per day, according to some reports, than any other Yankee. How many exactly? "We haven't really kept count," a weary Yankee PR person responds, with an edge that seems to question the asker's sanity. "Just a lot. A *lot*." They started coming the instant the twenty-year-old, born in New Jersey and raised in Kalamazoo, Michigan, stepped in early in the 1995 season, promoted from the Yanks' AAA minor leagues to fill a gap left by some injured players. In baseball parlance, Jeter was "up for a cup of coffee," not even lasting through the entire season in the majors—but his name and first impressions of his flashing bat and swift fielding did. Even after he was sent back to the minors, people kept asking for him, about him, writing to him. Columnists and professional sports watchers seemed as dazzled as the smitten young women and idolizing boys and girls who surrounded him outside the stadium before games, dashed down to the Yankees dugout for autographs during the game, and waited for a last meeting with him after each game was over. This public fascination has continued for three more seasons that have been full of greater achievements on the playing field and more and more widespread acclaim.

Tonight, the luster of the Yankees (and the promise of seeing Derek flushed and happy after a victory, the first of four in a clean sweep of the National League champs, the San Diego Padres) outshines even that of Hollywood. Many of the seats in the stadium tonight were filled with the rich, famous, and powerful. (In fact, according to some reports only a little over 5,000 seats were made available to the general public.) The fans waiting for their heroes react with curiosity but little ecstasy as multi-Oscar-winner Jack Nicholson passes, eliciting scarcely a glance, Yankee cap jammed low over his head. "Where's Derek?" one of the youngest girls plaintively wails, a big red paper heart blooming across her T-shirt. Then Calista Flockhart, Fox television's winsome attorney Ally McBeal, strides by nervously, thin as a rail, *her* face covered by a vintage Yankee cap. Flockhart doesn't hear a cheer, though, and the only commentary she arouses from the onlookers is "That girl needs to eat." Barbara Walters appears, handsome in a fall coat and big smile. "We won! We won!" the veteran TV reporter and headmistress of *The View* cries, giving a thumbs-up to the fans, who cheer and wave politely. "But where's Derek?" another girl asks anyone. "I have to go to the bathroom." Temperatures do rise a little for Sarah Michelle Gellar of *Buffy the Vampire Slayer* and movie star Bruce Willis. They almost reach high intensity when the short guy standing nearby chatting with a couple of cops turns out to be *Party of Five*'s Scott Wulf. He is the only nonbaseball celebrity anyone asks for an autograph that night.

Finally, the players begin to appear. If this were a normal Yankee night, they would approach the fans, sign autographs, maybe pose for pictures. But since it's the World Series, and since 800 policemen have been assigned to safeguard the players and public, and since the cops need something to do, they form a cordon a few feet away, keeping the players close but a little too far from their admirers. Everybody wails. One by one, to cheers and whoops, they appear: Wells, Tino Martinez (who walks up to the fans, smiles and waves, earning extra squeals and whistles of delight over his very fine looks), Paul O'Neill. The cops swarm about eagerly, as awestruck as the kids jumping up and down behind them to get a better view of their team.

Then one person gasps "There he is!" and there, indeed, is Derek Jeter: a little tired but affable looking, walking easily through the crowd, waving back at the fans, who shatter the sound barrier with a cry of adoration. The boys and young men behind the barricades chant "DJ! DJ! DJ!" like soldiers on maneuvers. The girls and women (even the forty-something mother of one of them, oblivious to the stare of the man next to her, who happens to be her husband) go an octave above the males, in a long spiral of one sacred word— "DEEEEEERRRRRREEEEEEKKKKKK!"—that goes on for a solid minute, until their idol is out of sight. It probably would have continued, the howls piercing the chilly Bronx midnight, but for the sudden appearance of several dozen people rather sheepishly walking in front of us and into the buses reserved for the San Diego Padres. Adoration gives way to the merciless scorn New

Yorkers can dish out better than anyone else: "Losers! Losers!"

"Are you sure they're all with the Padres?" someone asks, to be answered by "Of course they are! Lookit all the blondes!" Once the San Diegans are cooling their heels (and lost hopes) on their buses, depression sets in. The game is over. Derek has left the building. Nobody got autographs.

It's a heady spell, after all. The New York Yankees are the greatest baseball team in the world. Tonight's World Series marks the start of their 35th attempt to win the World Series. They were successful 23 of those prior attempts. The last victory was in 1996, Jeter's rookie season, and he was no small part of that triumph. Their stadium, built in 1923, is not so much a sports venue as an historic shrine. Visiting teams enter it with a mixture of respect and defiance and awe. Generations of sports lovers have filled its seats season after season. The lives and words and achievements of its players, managers, and owners have fascinated those generations. It makes it all the more amazing, then, to look around tonight and see Derek Jeter's presence everywhere. Vendors can't stop selling Jeter memorabilia; despite the higher cost (Derek's name, signature, or player number on a shirt, hat, or other garment can raise the price by as much as five dollars) fans buy in bulk and come back for still more next time. There is something about this young man, beyond his sterling performance on the playing field, that has become the focal point of this seemingly unbeatable team of commanding, remarkably accomplished athletes. More than any other Yankee, perhaps, Derek Jeter exemplifies the power of that spell.

Journalists and baseball pros are awfully tough to con. With a generosity typical of sports lovers, they are quick to praise, but also careful to be measured with any enthusiasm. If an early flasher of a player doesn't live up to the promise of his initial impression, they say so. Jeter has seemed to them not so much a hot young player as a phenomenon, someone to be watched and written about with awe:

"In a Yankees–Indians game the other night, Derek Jeter made a play I've never seen before," wrote syndicated conservative columnist John Leo. "On a ground ball deep in the hole between short and third, he leaped high in the air and, while airborne, threw hard and accurately to first for the out. None of the shortstops in my rosy memories could have made that play."

"When [Derek Jeter] came up for good in 1996, [Yanks manager Joe] Torre hoped for .250 and defense," writes the *New York Post*'s sports columnist Joel Sherman (.250 being an okay batting average for a rookie quivering through his first major-league season). "But Jeter was a star from that Opening Day. He changed the entire talent level of the team as a middle infielder who can do it all. And he has just gotten better each year, adding a power component and becoming a superb defensive shortstop. His willingness to work at his craft, despite all the siren songs of fame that call him particularly, is emblematic of the whole team."

Civilian sports fans are just as enthusiastic over the young shortstop's performance—on and off the field. New York's former governor, Mario Cuomo, himself once a minor-league center fielder for the Pittsburgh Pirates, comments "I think what's unusual about Jeter is his collection of talents at this early age [24]—he plays like a guy who's been playing shortstop for 15 years. He does everything well, and he learns. As an athlete he's unusual, extraordinary—not unique perhaps. But beyond that is the way he deports himself. He has enough of the small boy in him to make him charming, but he is at all times civil, well mannered, living by the obvious manners."

Other fans have earthier reasons for admiring Derek: "He's so cute, he drives me nuts," says one. "I will marry Derek when I grow up," swears one of his teenage cheerleaders at the 1998 World Series victory parade. "I will. I *will.*" Other Jeter fans, overhearing her, make sour, competitive faces: Sharing the fantasy can get ugly.

And then there were the love letters tossed beseechingly at him during the 1996 ticker-tape parade celebrating the Yankee World Series win Jeter helped make possible. Not dozens of letters. *Hundreds.*

Jeter's colleagues haven't written him any love letters (that we are aware of) but express their approval just as ardently:

"This kid is amazing. He plays like a guy who's been around for 10 years," Phil Rizzuto, Hall of Fame Yankee and longtime Yankee broadcast announcer, raved to *Yankees* magazine about the shortstop's rookie season. "I'm trying to think who the best Yankee shortstop I've ever seen is and I keep coming back to this kid. He could turn out as the greatest shortstop the Yankees have ever had."

"He's like kid dynamite, he's got so much going for him," Yankee manager Joe Torre observed, with a little of the wonder almost everyone expresses when they begin to talk about Jeter. "He's a tough kid, both physically and mentally. That will enable him to do a lot of things."

"I watched him blossom into a major league shortstop," former Yankee third baseman Wade Boggs commented during the October 1996 run to the World Series—in Jeter's rookie season with the team. "He has exceptional talent. He has great tools. He does a lot of things real well. He's a quiet kid, but he'll be a veteran one day and step into the spotlight."

"He's a good shortstop," said New York Met Rey

Ordonez, during Jeter's rookie season. ''I think, with time, he's going to be the best shortstop in the American League.''

Yanks coach Willie Randolph: ''I'm telling you, this kid might be a rookie in name, but in mind, heart and ability, he's got to be a six-year veteran, because that's exactly how he plays.''

''His potential is unlimited,'' Cal Ripken, the future Hall of Fame shortstop, has said. And he ought to know.

Longtime baseballer Don Zimmer, a former shortstop himself and now a coach for the Yanks, expressed his professional opinion even more succinctly. The veteran of 50 seasons in baseball went over to Joe Torre one day during Jeter's stupendous rookie season with the Yankees and told him: ''We have found a treasure.''

On the other hand, ''He is the absolute worst at returning phone calls. He's always late,'' Alex Rodriguez, sovereign shortstop for the Seattle Mariners and said to be Jeter's closest friend in baseball, 'fessed to *ESPN The Magazine*. ''And he's a horrible basketball player. He thinks he's got mad game, but he has *no game*.'' Nobody's perfect.

Tonight, it's safe to say, Derek Jeter has hit a new peak of popularity; he still handles it as politely and professionally as ever. His simple human warmth and unassuming manner are as charming as his good looks. Millions of Americans know his smile and handsomeness from countless photos and video clips but, up close, he seems even more striking—taller and heavier than most shortstops (6'3", 195 lbs.), swift and graceful despite his size, with a broad face that, even confronting a siege of near-delirious shrieking females, seems friendly and poised. His eyes are a vivid, fresh green. His face seems like several all at once. Sometimes he looks like a shy, almost dopey kid, the eyes watching carefully beneath big lids, the mouth open slightly as if he's about to sigh yet again. Then someone says something, or he is made to laugh, and the face suddenly matures into that of a dashingly handsome young man. Then he calms down, appearing more thoughtful, looking off to the side maybe, and his eyes get mellower, serious, as if all the attention just has to be absorbed for an extra moment, to assimilate it. But, at last, he ducks his head and faces you again, this time with another welcoming if slightly shy smile.

Regular Jeter fans (the teenage girls who follow Jeter like extra shadows are sometimes called Jeterettes or Jetermaniacs) readily tell you how friendly and accomodating he is with them on nights when the cops, the superstars, and the world's media are not around. He gives autographs with the automatic dispatch of a player who could sign for fans in his sleep. In a Jeter close encounter, the recipients are awed, giggling with excitement, grateful, or just casually friendly. It's these last Derek Jeter responds to the most easily. Though he does an amazing job of appearing professional and prepared, being in the spotlight on and off the field isn't easy, even for someone who has mastered that talent at an relatively young age. He enjoys the attention, but there is something in the way he steps around people and waits an instant before responding to a question that makes you realize how seriously he takes his job, and how careful he has to be to live up to its expectations. At an age when others are just starting to figure out what they want to do with their lives and how to begin their journey, Jeter is already well along on a tough career under the watch of millions of constantly adoring but demanding eyes.

They have heard a lot about him. How he was born in New Jersey and moved with his family to the Midwest when still a toddler. How, on a summer vacation while staying with his grandmother in New Jersey, he was taken to a Yankee game, and decided then and there he wanted to be a member of that team someday. How he then methodically, steadily, and with an unnaturally mature determination, rapidly grew into a strong, talented young player worthy of that little boy's goal. And how he was drafted right out of high school by the Yanks, who promoted him with startling swiftness through the minors and then up to the majors, making his debut with the dream team at the amazing age of 20. And then how he helped the Yankees win the World Series in his debut season, and has become an ever more essential element in that team's prosperity ever since, his life off the field (including a romance with a major singing star) coming under as much public scrutiny as his achievements in Yankee Stadium.

They have heard all this. But the whole story, taken in one sweep, remains a remarkable one. Derek Jeter's is the story of a dream, a determination, and a confidence that, so far, has proven him capable of achieving amazing feats at a still young age.

The eyes outside Yankee Stadium tonight are getting tired. Several of the teenagers are yawning, and even the cops look like they want to head home. So after a few more waves and "I love you, Derek!"'s shouted into the night (in case he is still within earshot) everyone disbands. You wonder how someone who has just played baseball for four hours with the world avidly watching, someone who feels the competitiveness and desire lock on his bat swings, then somehow copes with all this adulation and performs up to its expectations, manages to go home and calm down enough to get a good night's sleep.

That makes you wonder more about Derek Jeter. It's fascinating to watch a person who has known all his life what he wanted out of it and pursued his goal with such singleminded devotion, and made of the dream and the effort a near-flawless success. When Jeter steps up to the plate in the Bronx, nearly a hundred thousand eyes gleam in a mixture of suspense and wonder over what he has already done, is about to do, and is. How on earth has it all happened—and will he keep making it happen . . . ?

Second Inning

The Dream

"Baseball made me."

It is a beautiful summer day at Yankee Stadium, and all through the stands you can see parents and grandparents sitting beside children of all ages. The toddlers rock in their seats and seem deaf to the explanations the adults chatter into their ears. The older kids already know the game, have their own caps and junior-size mitts. They wave pennants, and flip through the season yearbook, maybe arguing with adults over which pictured player is the better pitcher or shortstop. The game proceeds. We don't know who played against the Yanks that day, but let's say the home team won.

We'll assume that because, in light of why we are interested in this ballgame, a victory would fit in nicely with the rest of the story, for out there in the stands, naturally unnoticed by anyone else, sits a six-year-old who, in a little over a decade, would be on the premises, but not in the bleachers with other fans: Instead, the crowd would be roaring approval for his expert playing and passion for the sport. The six-year-old would become a member of that team and a crucial figure in the Yankee present and future:

Derek Sanderson Jeter, visiting the East from his home in Kalamazoo, Michigan, is attending his first baseball game, and the dream of his life is about to begin.

He is visiting his maternal grandparents for the summer, and his grandmother, Dot Connors, a passionate baseball enthusiast, has taken little Derek to the Bronx. It is the six year old's first live game, but it won't be the last; Dot Connors and one of Derek's uncles will continue to treat him to these events that will eventually define his life. She is probably the ideal adult to bring this particular little boy to the Yankees, for Dot has been a devotee of this team for much of her life. Her love of the game is not only visceral (enjoying the setting, the velocity of the plays, the cries of the crowd) but historical. She has an accumulation of stories about the Yankees, their great stars and victories, which she relishes sharing with her little grandson, who already has the alert, lovely green eyes, the expressive, eager face, and open manner that, a few years later, will make him an outstanding player himself and a figure of admiration and fantasy for millions.

This ordinary summer outing was the turning point in the life of Dot's grandson and (it is beginning to be clear) the life of the team she loves and little Derek is learning to love: for watching the Yankees play, he has said, made him discover his vocation. He left that game and went back to West Milford, New Jersey, where he spent the summer with his grandparents and, not long after that, knew what he wanted out of life: the thin blue pinstripe uniform, the navy blue cap with a thickly sewn "NY" crowning the front (instantly recognizable as the sign of a champion to anyone who knows baseball), the proud stance at home plate, the firm batter's swing, the fielder's magnetic rush to the ball, and the shouted approval of 57,000 fans.

Not very many of us figure it all out so quickly. Finding what we love about being alive, and trying to learn if we can do that thing well enough to be praised and rewarded for it, is a tough process. Many people have to spend the first two or three (or even four) decades of their lives slugging through . . . and often we come up short at the end of the quest. What we love might not be something we're good at. Or we'll spend a lifetime thinking we are going after that perfection, and when we hold the achievement in our hearts, we discover it is not what we wanted or needed to be totally ourselves, after all.

When he entered the stadium that day, Derek was already indoctrinated in Yankee lore. William and Dot Connors had entertained their visiting grandson with Yankee games on television in New Jersey. And Dot herself seems the kind of fan rich with appreciation for the sport and the team; she had the ability to communicate both to her eager grandson. *Sports Illustrated* reporter Kelly Whiteside described the sense of Yankee history Derek's grandmother has: "In her day, Dot likes to say, it didn't get any better than turning on the radio and hearing the sound of Joe DiMaggio's bat meeting a hanging curve ball." In 1948, she was one of the throngs of New Yorkers who somberly paid respects to the ultimate Yankee, Babe Ruth, joining the long line of mourning fans filing past the late baseball giant's coffin resting at home plate. Though still a child, Derek was already accumulating his own baseball lore, such as the day he waited in a parking lot for an autograph from his great idol, star of the New York Yankees and the San Diego Padres, Dave Winfield.

Later, when the boy was a man (and a Yankee) this process of talking the history continued. The joy this gave to the grandmother can be easily imagined: Her dreams of great baseball games became Derek's. Now, others dream of *him*, and his great plays will encourage members of the next generation to dedicate themselves to the sport.

For every generation, the dream is widely shared, but the realization of that dream can be frustratingly elusive. At this point in his childhood, Derek was just another sports-struck kid. It is very hard to make that enthusiasm last, to translate it into real, reliable skills and emerge from all that effort the baseball player of your own and everyone's dreams.

These high odds against fulfillment make Derek Jeter's story even more remarkable. It's a key reason the ballplayer holds, for his wide, appreciative public, such intense fascination: everyone wants to ask him, in one way or another, "How did you *do* this?"

In his case, the primary answer is simple. In addition to being gifted, Derek Jeter has also been very, very lucky. He had the seemingly perfect family for a child with his gifts. They provided him with the natural ability, the security to look outside himself for what would complete him as a person, and the support and reliability to help him go as far as his talents could take him.

The baseball gift comes, curiously, from both sides of the family. He inherited his prowess on the field, no doubt, from his father, Dr. Charles Jeter, a psychologist who is a passionate sports fan and was shortstop for his college baseball team. The passion for the game comes from the mother's side as well, from Dorothy Jeter (Derek's mom), an accountant, and her mother, Dot Connors, who, as we've already seen, struck the spark that began the chain reaction of hard work and play that built a great sports career.

"I won't brag about me," Derek Jeter has said, "but I'll brag about my family forever."

The story of Derek Jeter must start with them, because it seems almost everyone who has had close encounters with the athlete, both on and off the baseball diamond, agrees on one thing: This guy must have remarkable parents.

"He has a foundation from his parents," stated Yankee coach Willie Randolph to the *Bergen Record*. "He's known from an early age how important it is to handle it, when maybe some other guys didn't."

"They've always been very supportive to their kids," says Don Zomer, a teacher in the Kalamazoo, Michigan, public school system and Derek Jeter's baseball coach at Kalamazoo Central High School. "Supported them 100 percent."

"Derek is a perfect example of what his parents taught him," a close friend and colleague, Yankee Jorge Posada, told the *Bergen Record*'s Tara Sullivan. "He's very humble. Even with all the fanfare, he's still on an even keel. You always get the true Derek when you meet him, and that tells a lot about a person. And you can see how much he appreciates his parents."

Throughout the raising of their two children (Derek's sister, Sharlee, five years his junior, now attends college in Georgia), the Jeters demonstrated remarkable attentiveness and skill. They had no idea, when Derek Sanderson Jeter was born on June 26, 1974 in Pequannock, New Jersey, what they were getting into. (Raising any child isn't easy; raising a little prodigy can be next to impossible.) But, it's likely, considering what we know about them, that they wouldn't have altered their course if they had been let in on what the future would bring to their son and his family.

Charles and Dorothy demonstrated strength of character by their own marriage. Charles Jeter is African-American; Dorothy Connors Jeter is of Irish descent. They married in one of the most tempestuous moments in American history: the tail end of the Civil Rights movement, the decades-long series of boycotts, demonstrations, protests, rallies, voting-rights initiatives, and riots that began the process of shaking America out of its longstanding tolerance of racism.

When the Jeters married, they were in effect breaking the law in some parts of the country in which interracial marriages had long been illegal. (Actually, it is still illegal to marry out of one's own race in some parts of America. A recent referendum to overturn such a law in South Carolina passed, but 38 percent of the voters wanted to retain the old law.) Their cute baby boy would have been considered evidence of miscegenation, the sexual coming together of two races that many Americans, for decades of our history, considered immoral and a threat to the social and moral welfare of the country. Such a child was usually called a *mulatto*, a term that is still hurled as an insult at the products of such marriages. Today, they are more respectfully called *biracial*, *multiracial*, or *of mixed race*. (There are, of course, still those Americans who hold to less enlightened views to this day. Since some baseball lovers are unaware of the player's racial background, maybe a few of them are even Derek Jeter fans.) Biracial marriages, which laws and customs made rare occurrences, were beginning to increase by the early 1970s; in some parts of the country, tolerance for such marriages was expressed. But still, what a lot of guts it must have taken in that time and place for this young couple to pledge their lives to each other. (It's a pledge that has held: The Jeters are still together.)

Even when able to find a tolerant environment, the parents and children of such a union faced great risks. The courage and openmindedness of such a family can threaten less-secure neighbors, sometimes entire communities. Hostility to an interracial marriage is not limited to whites: People from all sides of America's racial divide can find such unions, and the children they produce, disturbing. They remind some of the long history of oppression (ownership, brutality, segregation, political and social and educational exclusion) visited against blacks by whites, and remind others of the enormous strides toward equality—and competition—made, despite massive impediments, by African Americans.

Children, especially, can be singled out by white or black kids as targets by peers who can quickly pick up (and act upon) the casually passed-down prejudices of their parents.

Yet, among many remarkable facts in Derek Jeter's life story is this: He claims to have suffered little, maybe not at all, from being the child of a white mother and black father.

Jeter's attitude toward the racial issues his history embodies has always been a clear one: He has stated, again and again, that he felt little trouble from it while growing up. He claims he has often been mistaken for a Latino, because of his tan complexion and bright eyes.

"Racial problems?" says Jeter high school baseball coach Dom Zomer. "As long as I've known the Jeters, there has never been a problem with that. Derek has said he can get along with anyone—get along with the white kids, the black kids, even the Hispanic kids, because he is often taken for one. Derek's seen his biracial background as an advantage."

"It was never an issue," recalls one of Derek's grammar school teachers, Shirley Garzelloni. "Our schools have been integrated for some time. We're kind of an inner-city school with students of many different ethnic backgrounds."

Jeter himself has always demonstrated a remarkable ability to interact with nearly anyone. Watch him when greeting fans: with the parents he is respectful but witty; with young people he can be jocular and charming, more like a peer than a famous older person. It is impossible to detect any time when the race or gender or age or, in fact, any part of the identity of the other person touches something to alter his manner, or move him to distance himself. He must possess some of the preconceptions every person has, but his personable manner is a good demonstration of how a person in a society made of people drawn from the entire world should behave. Whether this ability was a characteristic he was born with, or another gift from his parents, or something he simply acquired himself, he alone can say. What is important is that this quality be noticed, and encouraged in others.

Jeter's own success has been part of a sudden wave of achievement from mixed-race Americans, as the children of the civil-rights era reach adulthood and begin making their own mark: Derek joins such famous figures in their own fields as Mariah Carey and Tiger Woods, among others. Inevitably, as Jackie Robinson (the first African American to break the color barrier in the major leagues) became a role model for many blacks and whites eager to overcome their troubled mutual history, Jeter, Carey, Woods, and others are now starting to assume these roles—and responsibilities.

In terms of his own behavior, however, Jeter has demonstrated awareness of social problems and a commitment to addressing them. Near the end of his rookie season, acclaimed on all sides as a major new player, at a moment when any young star could be forgiven for focusing on the money and adulation just another game away, Derek (with the help of his father) was founding the Turn 2 Foundation, a not-for-profit group that raises money to assist organizations and programs helping young people with substance abuse and other problems.

"He has a lot of respect for people," Joe Torre observed. "There's no question he has had some great upbringing."

This awareness and maturity are aspects of Jeter constantly noticed by others. Again, they came from his family. When Derek was four, the Jeters moved from New Jersey to Kalamazoo, Michigan, where Dorothy Jeter worked as an accountant for Upjohn Pharmaceuticals (a company that also has offices in New Jersey). Her husband became a therapist specializing in substance-abuse issues. Now with two children, the busy parents put their energies into raising them.

Friends and neighbors noted early on the devotion and strength they displayed. Derek attended St. Augustine's (a Roman Catholic parochial grammar school), and his parents quickly impressed on him the importance of learning, discipline, and effort.

He must have learned quickly because, even as a little kid, adults around him noticed the very qualities he would use to such profit as a baseball player. "I remember him as the kind of student that every teacher would want to have," says Shirley Garzelloni, who taught Derek when he was in the fourth grade. "He was always willing to help out, and help others. If there was a child who needed help with his work, you could pair him up with Derek. He had a way of assisting people without letting them know they needed it."

Mrs. Garzelloni, who has recently retired after 17 years of teaching at St. Augustine's, had been reminded of Derek's year in her class because of a discovery she recently made while cleaning out her desk at the school. There, somehow preserved for nearly 15 years, was the grade book for her 1983–84 class. "I went though it, and found the name—Derek Jeter, number eleven in the class list. And, my gosh, there isn't a single bad grade." Mrs. Garzelloni sees a direct correlation between this class record and the way, as she puts it, her former student gives "150 percent in baseball." She's also aware this story may sound suspect to a few listeners:

"When I talk about Derek to others, I sometimes

hear, 'Oh, come *on*—he can't be *that* good!' They're wrong. The person I see interviewed on TV is the same person I taught in the fourth grade. He was like an adult in a child's body.''

And he already knew the dreams he would make real as an adult. His teacher vividly remembers her student talking about becoming a Yankee—not maybe someday, but *definitely*. Because of his hard work and honesty, she was prepared to believe him, even then. ''Why should I have doubted him?''

''Derek *expected* that to happen someday,'' she goes on, ''but he seemed to think everybody should be in the same place, should be able to realize their dreams. He never flaunted his ability or his qualities.

''He was studious, with a great sense of humor, but he wasn't one of those goody-goody kids. Never tried to 'play' me as a teacher—no, no! I don't mean he didn't goof around the way other kids do, but that kind of behavior wasn't the norm for him.''

She was so aware of Derek's Yankee ambitions that she frequently kidded him about it. ''He would say 'Someday, I'm going to play for the New York Yankees,' and I'd say 'Well, that will make my husband happy, because that's his favorite team!' ''

The teacher never felt Derek was being pushed by parents driven by high ambitions for their son. ''They didn't ask from Derek anything he couldn't give back. If Derek came home and said 'I got a B,' his parents were the kind that would say 'If you did the best job you could do, that's great!'

''The best job—that's what they asked of both their children,'' Mrs. Garzelloni concludes. ''It wasn't the high mark that mattered to them, it was the level of application.''

All these attributes and Derek's application focused with impressive results when it came to baseball. Jeter recalls being about four or five years old when he got his first baseball mitt, so he was, like most boys, interested in the sport. But it seems pretty clear that baseball was not the *focus* of his young life until his visit to Yankee Stadium.

What we do know is that after that visit he began to prepare, with an almost unnerving precision, for his baseball career. While still very young, he would say "I'm going to be a Yankee" to people. This isn't that unusual: Most of us grew up wanting to be the hero of one sport or another. So what was it about this little kid from Kalamazoo that was so (no other word for it) radical?

For starters, he simply loved the sport. From the beginning, when he was a pint-sized grammar schooler, posing for his first of many "at bat" portraits, a home run expression on the sweet face undone by the big hair above it looking like it's about to send the baseball cap it stuffs springing into space, it was clear that the baseball diamond was home to him. And he acted on it as comfortably, and assuredly, as anyone would act in their home.

"The baseball field was his own little world," his father told the *Bergen Record*'s Rafael Hermoso a decade and a half later, when his son had just completed his rookie season by helping the Yanks win the World Series. "He just feels good out there. You might not see it, but his enthusiasm, his joy, I can look back and see the same mannerisms from Little League."

Derek's maternal grandmother knew this love firsthand. During his summer visits in West Milford, she related to *Sport's Illustrated*'s Whiteside, her grandson the Yankee would be up at dawn. "All his cousins would still be sleeping," she remembered, "and [Derek] would say, 'C'mon, Gram, let's throw.' Even as a little kid his throw would almost knock me over.''

Fortunately, Derek Jeter's calling was an accessible one for a little boy. You can't do much at seven or eight towards attaining your life goal if you want to be a politician or a nuclear physicist, except for shaking hands and blowing up things. But baseball, hey—every boy in the country has to step up to home plate and prove his stuff at least once between kindergarten and high school graduation. Happily, in our own day this is increasingly true for every *girl*, too, Derek's sister Sharlee (''A better shortstop than I am,'' according to her brother) among them.

It is not known whether Derek told his parents about his dream before or after they enrolled him in Little League. With that family background, it probably would have been impossible for him to get out of Little League unless he loathed it and it made him break out in a rash. But, since he was already at the point of being so in love with baseball and the Yankees he would lie awake at night dreaming about his future in blue pinstripes, Derek probably would have broken out if they hadn't let him play the game.

There are an estimated three-million-plus young people in the Little League at any given time. All 50 states have them. This estimate includes the 87 other countries that also have leagues. Baseball thrives in Japan (the hiring of Japanese pitcher Hideki Irabu by the Yankees became a milestone for his fellow countrymen), and in Cuba (Orlando ''El Duque'' Hernandez left there in hopes of playing pro in the U.S.A.), and in India, and even exists a bit in Europe, despite longstanding resistance to this thoroughly American sport. To run all these Little Leagues and help the kids become—potentially— great ball players, a million volunteers give time to the over 7,000 leagues set up for young people. Then there is the Babe Ruth League, which has close to a million players participating in over 6,000 leagues, and which emphasizes "team spirit" over winning.

This is more than a game—it's a huge, globe-spanning army of dreams, competition, and achievement. Each league has to play at least a dozen games a season. Williamsport, Pennsylvania, annually hosts the Little League World Series. Derek Jeter couldn't have started out in a better place: It has been estimated that 80 percent of all professional baseball players are Little League graduates.

Jeter, at first, probably didn't look very different from his fellows on the field, lots of whom loved the sport, too, and probably had their own fantasies of baseball stardom. So what made the difference? Two elements: natural ability, and (again) his parents.

Let's go to the second: From the first Derek's family encouraged him. Observers at even this stage confirm they were admired for their ability to nurture and challenge their kids. They had the gift not only of love, but further gifts of intelligence and discipline; and they made sure their son knew he had plenty of both, too.

A Kalamazoo resident who knew the family well describes how closely and carefully the Jeters worked with their kids: "Before every school year, the Jeters would sit down with Derek and Sharlee and come up with goals for the kids to accomplish: what kind of grades they should get, what clubs they would join, how much time they would spend studying, how much time in extracurricular activities. And if the goals weren't made there would be no baseball for Derek." This strategy apparently worked, for the observer continued: "I don't recall there was ever a time when Derek wasn't allowed to play baseball."

Derek had a prime coach in his family as well: His father had played in college and, when Derek needed to learn the sport, his dad made sure he knew every move in it. And his mother was as instrumental in helping him get started, too.

"My folks taught me at a very young age that there may be people who have more talent than you do," Derek told *Yankees* magazine, "but there's no excuse for anyone to work harder than you do—and I believe that."

The parents seem to have instinctively realized that Derek's best option would be to be good at every aspect of his sport.

"It seems a lot of parents would encourage one part of the kid's game," Dr. Jeter recalled later to Rafael Hermoso. "I wanted him to be an all-around player." He encouraged his son to develop as many baseball skills as possible, explaining that to be a shortstop, "you have to have more range."

Why shortstop? Derek offers the obvious explanation: "My dad had been a shortstop when he was in college, and, you know, when you're a kid, you want to be just like your dad."

"Shortstop has always been his position," Dr. Jeter told the *Kalamazoo Gazette*'s Paul Morgan, who has followed Jeter probably longer than any other sports writer. "He pitched a little in Little League and in a few junior varsity games, but short is where he's always wanted to be."

Derek's dad had attended Fisk University in Nashville, Tennessee, on scholarship, and played shortstop for their baseball team. (Although he did not receive an athletic scholarship: Charles Jeter graduated with a degree in Business Administration—the same major his son later pursued during his brief college career.) Like many elements in Derek Jeter's life, this one seems almost fateful—the guy who became one of the greatest shortstops of his day was lucky enough to have a shortstop father. Still, Dr. Jeter has said he didn't want his son to follow his sports career, and he didn't push short-stop on Derek, "but it was a position I knew and played, so it was a position I could teach him."

This must have taken a lot of patience, but Derek's father was, by training, a person skilled at helping others. In Michigan, he received a master's degree in Social Work as well as a doctorate in Philosophy, both earned from Western Michigan University. His principal work has been in clinical and private practices, working with patients (both adults and teenagers) dealing with emotional and substance abuse issues. To put it simply, years of work in the social services field, coupled with his fatherly solicitude, made him one serious coach.

And he knew and loved baseball just like his son. His favorite team was the Detroit Tigers. (Reportedly, Dorothy Jeter's favorite team was, needless to say, the Yankees; their son now tells interviewers with a smile that the whole family now has no choice but to be Yankee fans.) Dr. Jeter had kept a scrapbook of his clippings and mementos from his college days. When his son began to show prowess as a shortstop, he would bring out the scrapbook and show him these souvenirs from his time at Fisk.

At the time, Derek must have found the scrapbook of clips fascinating, for he still remembers going through it. Growing up, he was also encouraged to keep his own souvenirs of sports and academic records, as was his younger sister, Sharlee. But today, with tons of clippings of his own to save, he has been known to kid his father for the skimpiness of that old scrapbook—which consisted only of a few pages!

The youngster's enthusiasm and speed on the ball field must have been further inducements for him to concentrate on shortstop. Shortstop is the crucial defensive position in baseball. With more right-hand batters than lefties, most of the infield chances will be handled by the shortstop. A shortstop is responsible for intercepting anything that comes his way. He must be able to cover the whole left side of the infield and move into the outfield for popups, as well as for cutting off throws from the outfield. A shortstop needs every skill a ball player has: excellent timing and reflexes; strong but quick legs, to run to the ball instantly; good hands; a strong arm. A good shortstop must be able to make all the routine plays—and a high percentage of extraordinary ones. True shortstops with all these attributes—speed, aim, throwing, timing—are prized, so much so that their batting skills are often judged to be sufficient even if their averages are barely adequate. (Jeter quickly established himself as a far better hitter than that.)

However, even the father's own gifts as a shortstop (and the son's eagerness to follow in his footsteps) wouldn't have been enough to ensure Derek a fruitful career in that position unless he had demonstrable skills. The amazing thing was, he did.

Let's back off from the second reason to the first: natural ability. By the time Derek was well along in grammar school, his baseball gifts were obvious. People were already noticing, watching, and talking about this kid and the magic he could make on the field. Don Zomer, who would eventually be Derek's high-school baseball coach, was prepared for the player he'd teach. He hadn't known Derek during his early baseball seasons, but "I'd known *of* Derek for years, because everyone in Kalamazoo had heard about this fantastic Little League ballplayer."

When asked the obvious question—what did they see that was so special?—Zomer, who has taught baseball for close to a quarter-century in Kalamazoo, and knows a good player when he sees one, remembers the young Jeter very clearly. And the excitement of what he saw accelerates and warms his voice.

"Derek has *always* had what it takes to be a good ball player. First of all, he had that fantastic arm. And he's got all the other things that go with it: the foot speed, the quick hands for good fielding, the quick bat."

Zomer first saw him play in a summer all-star program for baseball players. Jeter was first with the Mickey Mantle League, which was for younger all stars. (Derek was 14 at the time.) "In Mickey Mantle, they had him playing third base. He was an instant star. He's always played one step ahead of where his age group was; and he still does." Jeter then moved to the older, Connie Mack League (up to 18 years), playing for a Kalamazoo team called the Maroons. Zomer stresses that the playing standard in these leagues was very high— Kalamazoo is proud of its kids and their abilities—and that even in this atmosphere, Jeter just shone. "It was so obvious. Even then."

And Derek must have been something to watch. He seems to have been the kind of student who doesn't gradually acquire certain skills as he does rapidly grasp them, master them, and quickly turn them to his own uses. Coaches, parents, players must have been amazed as this otherwise normal-looking kid stepped up to Little League and high-school home plates, gotten into a junior version of the Jeter crouch his present-day admirers know well (looking like a V on its side, bat tip wiggling above his head) and prepared to bat. The face probably changed pretty much the way it does now, sharpening with concentration. Then that concentration flashed to energy: He'd swing with precocious sureness and, while people were watching the ball head into the air, its young batter became a human blur, wanting nothing so much as to tear through the space and bases separating him from his goal, *the* goal: the score waiting at home plate.

Even the opposing team must have enjoyed watching him.

(When talking about his natural abilities, it should be added that a flair for sports seemed to be shared among the Jeter clan: aside from his Dad's baseball credentials, Derek is second cousin to two pro-football players, Gary Jeter, former defensive end for the Giants, and Eugene Jeter.)

The kid was clearly prodigious, but all this took an enormous amount of work. Maybe *work* isn't the best word: *dedication* fits Derek Jeter better. When he plays he is having a great time, but what's going on clearly means more to him than a game. Perhaps this is why so many Jeter watchers, even hardened professionals, instinctively think of baseball history when they write or speak of him. (Even a clever fourth-grader visiting Yankee Stadium during a World Series game caught this feeling, smiling and waving at Jeter after the game and turning to her father—who understood what she meant perfectly—to say "He's like a history lesson.") Make no mistake: It wasn't easy. "He's had many hardships and setbacks along the way," a Kalamazoo friend says, "but he kept at it." Sometimes his dream must have seemed stubbornly elusive. His family helped him stick to his purpose. Two incidents illustrate their support:

A grammar-school Derek is at bat in the middle of a Little League game, and that description of him causing pure rapture at the bat four paragraphs ago is *not* happening. As he recalled the incident to writer Tara Sullivan early in his amazing 1998 season, he had already swung twice at "two terrible pitches," putting him behind, with the count at 0 and 2. Then the ball approaches, and he hears the dreaded words: "Strike three!" The future Yankee genius has been struck out, and he's *pissed*. No dreams of glory in the air today—rather, some angry muttering, "It's a bad call," probably over and over, until he makes it back to his team's bench.

He bemoans the strikeout to his dad (who apparently was there): "Bad call," "Way out of the zone," and so on. Dr. Jeter listens and responds "You just swung at the two pitches before. Why would you complain about the umpire? Control what you can control." Two crucial lessons here, one technical (*don't* swing at any pitch— a lesson the young ball player still forgets now and then in his eagerness to score); the other, larger and harder to enact, about baseball and life. People who focus on themselves and what they do and how they do it tend to get more out of life than those who don't.

"He knows what to do and keeps his emotions down," Dr. Jeter concluded to Paul Morgan. They were talking just as Derek was launched into his first Major League World Series, when many wondered how the rookie, even *this* rookie, could possibly handle the Series and its brutal pressures. "I would never bet against him, though. When someone says he can't do something, he will prove them wrong. He's very competitive."

The second story is more remarkable. Dom Zomer recalls coaching Jeter one afternoon after high school. Practice completed, the team heads home; the coach does too. After dinner, Zomer returns to Kalamazoo Central for some kind of school meeting. It's dusk, and as he drives up to the school he sees four people on the baseball field. It's the Jeters.

It's not the only time he saw them; so did others. They lived, at that time, next door to the high school, one side of their property adjacent to the school ballfield. After their dinner, they would climb over the fence with their own baseball equipment, and coach Derek. He would practice hitting, or they would hit grounders to him. Baseball was not just a sport Derek was good at: It was another way of being part of his family.

To this day, he generates that family feeling on the ballfield and in the dugout, despite players of many different backgrounds, with different salary packages (and agents) and agendas. He generates it when talking to sports reporters, who sheathe their aggressions and almost always listen respectfully as he fields their questions. And we have already glimpsed how his fans benefit from this security of his, of knowing where he is and what he is doing.

Baseball may have been Jeter's ambition, but it wasn't his entire life. He was in many other respects a conventional kid. He lived a full schedule of school, games, and family activities. At St. Augustine's, he remained a fine student and, when he graduated to Kalamazoo Central High School in 1988, his impressive academic record continued. Teachers remember him fondly for being a smart kid who didn't fit the usual "jock" mold: He was interested in much more than baseball. He had a very quick, ready mind, and in school reports and theme papers he expressed himself well. When graduating grammar school he was asked, for posterity, what he wanted to be . . . you can guess the answer. It's telling that there seem to be few instances of adults and peers hearing the adolescent say "I want to be a Yankee when I grow up" (and he has said he used to announce that a *lot*) and answering it with "Oh, sure. Right." or one of those other flip phrases adults can use to puncture young dreams. People seemed to have known this was a fantasy with a foothold in reality. In an eighth-grade creative-writing assignment, he wrote of his Yankee future. The teacher, Chris Oosterbaan, didn't find anything fantastic about the hopes. "That is what he predicted and we didn't laugh at it either. You could take what he said seriously."

More important, the builder of the fantasy seems to

have known it: If Derek had doubts, they didn't get in the way long enough to slow him down.

After Derek Jeter won the 1996 World Series as the New York Yankees' shortstop, he returned in triumph to Kalamazoo. People were struck at how unchanged he was—still the intense yet friendly, sincere person they went to school with, or taught.

Doug Biro, who first met Jeter in the fourth grade at St. Augustine's, remains his friend, and has described him as "the most honest person I know. His work ethic, with any aspect of his life, is remarkable."

Teacher and public-school administrator Mike Hinga agreed. "A lot of people are good," he explained to Mickey Ciokajlo, " a lot of people are great winners, but he's just truly a good person."

And a good student. Jeter's grade-point average was usually just below 4.0. The smart A-student normally would have been full of ideas for what kind of future he had. But he knew what he wanted, and his teachers knew he knew.

What must it have felt like for Derek to return to his high school only four years after graduation—not with a college degree (as most members of the class of '92 would), but a World Series ring and the roar of several million fans packing Manhattan's Canyon of Heroes in his ears? That day he was his usual affable self, meeting new teachers, greeting old ones, talking encouragingly to students. Some observers must have been amazed at how level a head he was maintaining, but those who knew him in those school years, and were close observers, wouldn't have been too surprised, because he handled success back then about the same way.

On his high-school team, Jeter may have been the standout in the lineup, but he never acted like a star. "Derek's not a boastful person, and he certainly wasn't then," his coach remembers. "As we talked as a team or in the locker room before and after games, Derek never centered conversation around himself. He was always focused on the *team.*"

That commitment to being a great *player* rather than a headliner persists to this day, Zomer adds. "Even today, when we talk about upcoming fundraisers for Kalamazoo Central High School, Derek wants to be involved in them—but he doesn't want the focus to be exclusively *on* him. He's not the only pro athlete from this high school, and he wants to include them in the plans. Just like when he played on our team."

But, he adds, Jeter's serious involvement in the sport was acknowledged among his colleagues. "It was just always known that this was his desire, to be a major-league baseball player."

(Jeter's parents shared his intense concern for the whole team: An observer recalls Dorothy and Charles Jeter's encouragement for all the other players: "His mom was always there to support the team in any way possible: went to all the games, made things for the team—not just Derek, the whole team. At games, the Jeters wouldn't just cheer Derek, but every player. Derek has done this all his life—supported the team he played for, because that's what his parents did.")

Mike Hinga echoes Zomer's recollections. He coached Jeter, too—for several years, on the Kalamazoo Maroons. This was a competitive team, playing about 80 games a summer. It was an all-star lineup, which means Derek wasn't the only player with dreams of baseball glory filling his head and honing his body. Nevertheless, even in this setting, Jeter was the standout for two reasons: He was the best player, and he didn't try to ride being the best.

"He's sincere," Hinga told Ciokajlo of the *Kalamazoo Gazette.* "That is not a front. If it is, I've never seen the front drop."

The modesty and earnestness certainly surprised Hinga. It's natural for anyone having a good game to strut and swagger: Some people *play* the sport for that opportunity. Part of being a good coach is knowing how to handle that swaggering when it starts getting in the way of winning, or keeping a team together. But Hinga declared "I don't think that existed for him."

Derek was already prepared for what the future was hurrying to bring him.

So were his parents. Derek was taught by them not only to be a good player, but a disciplined one. Right away, his family seemed aware that the son's talent and potential would require much more than the ability to catch and throw and hit well. By demanding a high academic performance and all-around responsible behavior, the Jeters spared their son a pro career full of personal and professional disappointments and embarrassment. Careers of brilliant potential have been ruined, or never given a chance to come to fruition, because other elements necessary to make a success of the sport—self-control, public manners, the ability to handle stress and surprise, and constant presence of mind— were insufficiently developed. Young athletic stars are urged to focus on their playing technique, when they should be studying other subjects, learning how to cope with ordinary life situations, and preparing for a stress-laden future (the better they are at the sport, the more stressful the future will be). Shrewdly, Dorothy and Charles Jeter didn't wait for some later coach to begin to instill the proper values into their son; they did it themselves. Without this family, it is clear Derek wouldn't have made it to where he is, or been able to handle the pressures of success so well.

Even great kids move through that phase of life where they have plenty of moments of rebellion, or awkwardness, or confusion. It's called adolescence, and even Derek Jeter endured it. In some photos from his teen years he looks a little sheepish about his height (at 17 he was 6'2"). His adolescent face bears an openness that often foreshadows the charm of the adult's—but sometimes he looks baffled at how much is happening to him so quickly. Even the increasingly smart-looking uniforms and caps can't disguise that beneath all the skill and ambition is a boy. And, at some point, every boy, even in the most nurturing of families, needs to push himself away, declare himself his own man.

Once, talking to a group of teenagers, Jeter told a few stories about his adolescent years. (He is probably at his best with such groups—with no adults around, he seems to relax and show more of the sense of humor his colleagues and friends often cite.) He would be bouncing a baseball off a wall of the Jeter home, practicing his catching skills. It would get darker, and his mother would call for him to come in. He'd keep playing. She'd call again: "Derek!" Soon a duel was going on between repeating sounds: the mother's cry (probably getting increasingly commanding) and the son's ball thump thumping from wall to mitt. Well, we know who won— he had to go in sometime—and when Jeter told this story he had the room full of teenagers laughing in sympathy. But it wasn't just a funny story: It illustrates how baseball simultaneously keeps him close to his home and family (since they taught it to him and love it as he does) yet also was quickly pulling him away from them—and it was soon to do so physically.

And then there was romance. He may have occasionally appeared the gawky teenager, but Derek had the *looks* in high school. Acne may mar complexions, ears may grow faster than the rest of one's head, but beautiful green eyes are beautiful green eyes. He was clearly conscious of his good looks (his smile in early pictures is the giveaway), and seems to have been popular. Dorothy

Jeter has remarked she became aware of the phone calls
her son began receiving from schoolmates, primarily female. Derek hasn't said much about those years, although he did tell another story, to the same group of
teenagers, about taking a girl out on a date and having
to escort her home before long because his curfew was
earlier than hers. Just hearing that one is mortifying; but,
again, as Jeter told it, it was full of humor.

It has been reported that one of his teachers, on at
least one occasion, reacted to Derek's flirting too much
with girls in class by committing the ultimate act of romantic sabotage: she called his mother. (Whether Derek
and this teacher remained on good terms has not been
reported.)

Derek's romantic life is probably the closest-kept secret he has and, until recent events, no one had much of
a problem with this personal privacy. He did date, and
he was reportedly seeing one Kalamazoo girl in particular as late as his first season with the Yankees. The
teenager remembered today seems to have been more
playful and intense off the field than romantic and re-
bellious.

His father, however, recounts a powerful moment in
the young man's life. Derek was not only a baseball
player: he was good at basketball, too. He played so well
he was even said to be considering a career at that sport
(perhaps in emulation of his idol Dave Winfield, a college basketball star)—until, in senior year of high
school, his team got beaten, really beaten. That supposedly put a stop to Jeter's hoop dreams.

He and his dad were both strong players, and they
went one-on-one frequently. They were both competitive, in sports, in games (checkers). "He beat me all the
time," Derek told Tara Sullivan. "That's why I'm so
competitive. He had no mercy on me, never let up on
me."

Finally, eighth-grader Derek said, "I can beat you, dad. I learned some new moves." His parents must have sensed this was a big moment—they played this crucial game on a basketball court at Western Michigan University, where Dr. Jeter earned his higher degrees and where Derek would be accepted himself a few years later. Mrs. Jeter went along, perhaps to referee. At the end of the game, Derek was the clear winner.

"Derek has always had that desire to be the best," Dr. Jeter commented. Now he was leaving his parents behind. He was developing so fast, the world was noticing.

The Jeters, coaches like Zomer and Hinga, and teammates weren't the only ones keeping an eye on the young shortstop. Baseball is a young sport, and a rich one. Players start and finish early; the body can't handle more than, say, three decades of the intense physical stress the game demands. And that's a best-case time frame: Careers of ten years or less, wiped out by injuries or sudden lapses in playing skill, are quite common. This means professional teams (minor and major leagues) need an ever-fresh supply of youngsters to win games and earn money for them.

By the time Derek Jeter was a senior at Kalamazoo Central High School, he was a prospect. Big-league teams must know what's happening in their sport on the high-school level (scouts have been known to do Little League), to snap up the most promising young players before another team or college does so. The teams employ scouts, prospectors with educated eyes quick to spot and assess a promising form on any ballfield. Scouts have to work quickly, evaluating the prospect in question and alerting their bosses in the front office. Not every promising player appeals to every team—the needs of that team are also taken into consideration. Strong hitters are always needed; but a pro team with a full roster of short stops already coming up in its minor leagues probably wouldn't have been that interested in someone like Jeter—except the scouts kept submitting ever-more glowing reports of Jeter's skills in fielding, and hitting, and running.

Another field with a professional interest in baseball talent was paying attention to young Jeter. "I personally started picking up on him at the end of his junior year in high school," says Paul Morgan of the *Kalamazoo Gazette*. "The whole staff had heard of Jeter when he was seven or eight years old. He was already a rising star: 'You have to go see this Jeter kid play,' and I'd think, yeah, sure—everybody has a nine-year-old whiz kid. In this business, we tend to make big deals out of talented kids, and then by 14 they get burned out or turned off.

"But we knew Derek had the skills, so as he started getting older, we started doing things on him. I remember watching the last game of his Junior year. He went 4-4, made every stop he had to, and I'm sitting there going 'Okay!' The range he had as a shortstop—at 16—was something. With his arm, he could play so far back it was almost like he was playing short-*left*!''

Jack Moss, sports editor of the *Kalamazoo Gazette*, reported almost a year before Jeter's graduation that the young player was already well within the sights of the Central Scouting Bureau, "an alignment of 35 major league team scouts." Scouts follow a grading system that places the potential of baseball candidates: A score of 50 is considered serious, a sign of certain interest from the majors. Jeter, who had just turned 17 a few weeks before, was already graded a 55. Certainly, he began his last year of high school knowing his life was about to change, and his world about to grow considerably.

"During Derek's senior season in the fall, he played

basketball and put down baseball,'' Morgan remembers. ''Central Scouting sent him tests in the fall, and he also had the SAT's and stuff. He knew pretty much he wanted to go pro, [but] seeing his parents with their academic backgrounds, they wanted him to have the college option, too.''

Bob Watson, until recently general manager of the New York Yankees, was the assistant general manager for the Houston Astros in 1992. They had first pick in the draft, to be held in June, and were very interested in Jeter—Watson himself flew to Michigan to watch the young shortstop at work.

''You could tell even then that he was an intriguing talent,'' Watson remembered for *Yankees* magazine. ''Just the instincts, the way he moved. There was something about him that didn't let you forget him.''

Actually, Derek didn't have an amazing final year in high school baseball. There had been a mishap—he had briefly hurt an ankle earlier in the season. One April afternoon, having done well in the first game of a double-header against Portage Central High School, Derek went running in the first inning for an infield hit, and then slipped by first base—with about 40 pro scouts in the stands, hanging on his every move!

At first he was afraid to try the ankle. It hurt. The dream was weeks away from reality, already materializing in front of him—and a wet first-base bag could have meant the end of it. Once he got up, it was clearly a sprain and not a fracture or torn ligament. He was okay. Out for three games, Derek admitted being afraid the injury would scare the scouts away. He found almost right away it did nothing of the kind—but this may have been his first experience with major-league pressure, with feeling not only the interest, but formidable expectations of baseball watchers.

He was also getting a taste of the antagonisms that

surface when competition is fought in earnest: His batting average that spring was .481, scoring four home runs, batting in 23, and stealing 12 bases. The average was down from the previous season's .557, which was a school record. He wasn't subpar at bat; he was getting walked by insecure pitchers. For a player hungry for that crack of his bat against the ball, being cheated of hits like that must have seemed a real insult.

Even that didn't matter—every part of his game was coming together, as if he already knew the major leagues were his life. Derek's throws to first base were reaching pro speeds of 83 miles an hour. "Even his outs were impressive," Coach Zomer insisted, praising the increasing authority of Jeter's batting skills. "Derek hit balls normal high school players just couldn't handle."

He was still captain of his team, as he was of his varsity basketball team, for which he had played for three years. Although he still expressed certainty in a career in baseball, it wasn't the only future he could imagine for himself. "I'm going to college at some point," he stated around this time. "I'd like to become a doctor," he added—once. In light of what happened in his senior year, it's not surprising he hasn't said that much (publicly) since.

If his final high-school baseball season wasn't perfect, he was winning awards, anyway. *Scholastic Coach Magazine* gave him the Gatorade Award for being Michigan's top player. The Michigan High School Coaches' Association named him their Player of the Year. He had already been named a top national athlete by *Baseball America Magazine*; *Collegiate Magazine* put together a national dream team and, for shortstop, the best they found was Derek Jeter.

College was very much on the minds of his family, and Derek could have attended (and played for) University of Miami in Florida, which was his first choice.

However, he then became interested in Western Michigan University's baseball team. It would have been a fine college choice, close to home and with good family associations (his father earned his higher degrees there). But, by spring of 1992, as Derek prepared to graduate with an A average, it was becoming clear that major league baseball was no dream: it was knocking at (maybe even *down*) their door.

There are 28 major-league baseball teams in America today. By spring 1992, 27 of them had already scouted Derek Jeter: studied his plays, talked to him to size up his character, made it clear the team they represented was watching, and interested.

That was the good, the very good, news. Here was the bad: The one team that hadn't scouted Derek Jeter was the New York Yankees.

There were other fine young players buzzing with anticipation over the big picks. Scouts were leaking word to the Jeters that Derek would probably be the fifth pick in the draft, which meant he would be signed by the Cincinnati Reds. This was good news, too—a fine team, and one of Derek's idols, Barry Larkin, was their star shortstop. But, as Derek told *Sports Illustrated*, "I thought I'd be stuck behind Barry Larkin." Still, it was pro baseball, and no telling what the future might bring . . .

Then, on May 30, 1992, just forty-eight hours before the draft, the phone rang at the Jeters'. It was a man named Dick Groch, another scout. Derek hadn't heard from him personally, he said, because he didn't want to intrude on his family's privacy, but he had been aware of young Jeter for a couple of years, and the team he represented certainly had heard from him about the shortstop's skills. Dick Groch scouted for the Yankees. Now, this was exciting news—but the Yankees were *sixth* to pick in the draft, and Derek had already been told he was most likely pick number five.

Kalamazoo, understandably, was in a state of excitement about all this; the nation's sports dealers were validating the community's support and belief in their young shortstop. Sportswriter Paul Morgan did some detective work and stirred up the heat, stating that sources close to the Houston Astros (first pick in the draft) were saying Jeter was likely to be their choice. It still wasn't the Yankees, but number one was certainly something.

A lot for a kid to handle, too. Playing was something he was well on the way to mastering, but *waiting?* Derek played it cool: "My dad talks to the scouts, agents, and front-office people," he assured Morgan. "It works out best. . . . I let him handle all that stuff and I play baseball."

On Monday, June 1st, 1992, at 1:00 P.M. in New York, the amateur draft for the major league baseball teams began. The Jeters awaited the news, along with hundreds of thousands of other followers and players and owners of baseball. Draft day can be thrilling: the future of baseball decided in 28 picks, 28 best-guesses, which often don't pan out.

Derek wasn't first pick, after all. The Houston Astros went with an outfielder, Phil Nevin from Cal State–Fullerton. The second, third, and fourth teams (Cleveland Indians, Montreal Expos, Baltimore Orioles) made their selections. Then the Cincinnati Reds named their pick . . . and it wasn't Derek.

But the next team, the Yankees, picked him.

Derek was the first high-schooler picked in the draft (21 of the 28 players were college students). He was only the third shortstop ever chosen by the Yankees in the first round of the draft. Now he would negotiate with the Yankees for a five-year contract, for a lot of money.

(In the 1991 draft, it was noted at the time, one player selected pulled a $1.5 million package.)

He had graduated from high school just the other day, and was three weeks short of his 18th birthday. Not that long ago, he would stand before the mirror in his bedroom and the reflection would become The Yankee of his dreams. Now that reflection had stepped beyond the mirror and become part of his real world.

"It was a dream come true," he said several years of pro playing and one World Series win later, "because this is what I always wanted to do."

"Hard to believe," said his grandmother Dot, remembering that day.

All of their efforts had paid off beyond most peoples' wildest dreams—but not Derek's. And, perhaps, his family's. When they hung up the phone that day, jubilant from the news, maybe when they looked around and saw some of the tokens of their passion for baseball and support for each other as a family—the Yankee momentos, the autographs, the father's shortstop clips, the son's awards and photos—it meant something new to them. Maybe Derek now no longer felt a witness to the Yankee history he and his grandmother would pitch to each other, but was a part of it.

He has said, "All I ever wanted was to play baseball." At an age when most people don't know what they want that evening, let alone over a whole lifetime, he was well on the way to getting his wish.

Third Inning

Confidence

"You don't have much time do much else except play ball..."

Why don't we take stock for a moment of what Derek Jeter had done, and what he would now be expected to do? He had already vaulted the early obstacles of childhood and youth with unusual determination, success, and energy. He had pursued his goal with a singlemindedness many found startlingly grown up for a kid from Kalamazoo (or anywhere). At 17, he was widely recognized as a major talent in the most competitive sports field in his country. The team that had inspired him in grade school and been the dream of his life to join had drafted him, beating out a crowd of other clubs that surely would have snatched the young player into their ranks if the Yankees had hesitated or changed their minds. For any person, let alone a Michigan teenager, this was an amazing achievement, more than many others can boast of in their entire lives. Jeter might have been expected to allow himself a good, long exhale.

In fact, his challenges as a baseball player were only beginning.

Just before the draft, when rumors of a high pick were swirling around him, Derek told *Baseball America* ''I was surprised to hear I'd be picked so high.'' The talk must also have started him wondering about what was

going to happen after that pick. He knew the broad out-
line of it—he and the Yankees would negotiate a contract, and he would be assigned to one of the
organization's minor-league teams. As a sports fan, he
must have read reports of young athletes striking lucrative deals with their clubs. Now, he and his family had
to consider the Yankees' offer, weigh their options, and
sign on the dotted line.

Derek had signed a letter of intent to study at (and
play for) the University of Michigan. According to
NCAA (National College Athletic Association) rules,
this meant he could not hire a sports agent to negotiate
the contract for him. The Jeters were, however, allowed
to receive advice from unpaid sports agents or advisors
(and they did, from Steve Caruso). Charles Jeter handled
the negotiations, which began immediately after the draft
and then continued, slowly, throughout the rest of June.
Despite the presence of the pro adviser, Dr. Jeter made
it clear that the family knew what they were doing and
were calling the shots. (Yet again, his own history
helped his son's career: Charles Jeter has a BA in Business Administration.)

At first, the two sides, half a continent away, com-
municated by phone and fax. Then, as Charles Jeter told
the *Kalamazoo Gazette*'s Paul Morgan, ''We got to the
point where we were close and we decided to have them
make the trip here to close the whole thing.''

So, while Derek was playing his final summer games
for the Kalamazoo Maroons (not only shortstopping but,
on his 18th birthday, pitching a few innings), Dr. Jeter
was facing down the trio of Yankee negotiators, one of
whom, Dick Groch, was the scout that alerted the Yankees to Derek's abilities.

Contracts for a beginner usually cover several seasons, and detail not only salary and bonuses but plans
for the new player's development. With Derek there was

another consideration: his education. The Jeters were still convinced he needed a college degree. (Although Derek's expressed ambition to be a doctor vanished; eventually, he would take courses in business administration.) They were also savvy enough to know the Yanks' current interest in their son might not last forever; or he might be injured and disabled on the minor league fields, and unable to continue his career; or Derek himself might, after a season or two, decide that full-time pro ball wasn't the life for him after all. Such a decision is actually not so uncommon: A veteran scout once wistfully admitted some of the greatest young baseball players he ever discovered lost interest and never made it to the major leagues.

The Jeters, therefore, insisted the Yankees pledge a stake in their son's future, whatever it would be—on the ball field or in a profession. They made a condition of the deal that the Yankees agree to put Derek through college. It was a shrewd demand, and the organization agreed to it. The Yankees also made it clear to the Jeters that they were not signing their son as a quick fix, or to sell him to their public as an overnight sensation. Their plan was to slowly bring Derek up through the minors, no doubt convincing the parents they were dealing with a management that also had Derek's best interests in mind.

The deal was closed by June 28, 1992 (Derek had turned 18 two days before). Financially, it was certainly handsome for a middle-class Kalamazoo family: the package was worth $800,000. Derek received a signing bonus of $700,000. "We wouldn't have consummated the deal if we didn't feel good about it," Dr. Jeter admitted after the signing.

"I'm happy with the package," Derek enthused to Morgan, "and it's the most anyone has gotten in the first round,'' demonstrating a financial awareness that would bode well for his future.

The process must have been agonizing, not only because sports negotiations are not known for their civility, patient discussion, and all-around goodwill, but because the Jeters knew that, in doing the best for their son, they were also losing him. As soon as the contract was signed, Derek would be on his way to join the Yankees minor league team in Tampa, Florida. "The last couple of days we've come to the realization that we're closing a deal and we want to do what's best for Derek," Dr. Jeter said. Their deal would determine the next few years of their son's life; for those years, he would be away from them, a busy professional in a brutally competitive sport at an age when most sons and daughters are just beginning to learn to live on their own in sheltered, academic settings.

"They were nervous as all get-out," Paul Morgan remembers the Jeters about this time. "Not nervous he would fail, just normal kid-going-to-college nervous. They knew he would be well taken care of."

"If anybody every saw that family together," Shirley Garzelloni notes, "they could understand how hard it must have been to leave them. Derek's so much the big athlete—but there's still some of the little boy in him."

However hard, his parents knew this was what Derek wanted, and so it was what they wanted. And so, on June 30, their son left Kalamazoo for Tampa, where he was to play his first professional baseball game—in two days.

In high school, no matter how competitive he was, and no matter how hard he worked, Derek was still a student, and a son. "All I ever wanted was baseball," he'd said, and "One day I'm going to be a Yankee"—but he was still a player with a family to go home to, and homework to do, and summer vacations, and friends to have fun with. Now, he was a professional. The Yankees were investing a million dollars in outright money (over several years in their minor leagues) and more in terms of effort to provide the training and opportunities the young shortstop would need to reach the expectations the organization's coaches, managers, other players, and money men had of him. Jeter was now in baseball, which also means in business.

There are 19 minor leagues in America and, within each, there are numerous teams. A major league organization like the New York Yankees will operate several. There is the A, or entry-level team, for the greenest recruits, whose only baseball experience was restricted to amateur sports (Little League, varsity teams, and so on). The next level (AA) is where beginners can prove they are quick to learn and ready to advance to Class AAA, just a step from the major-league team.

Basically, Derek Jeter was walking into a world where everyone was working as hard as he was to realize their dreams—or trying to hold onto them—and where lots of money was at stake. Even in their training manifestations, the ultimate goal of a pro ball team is to make money—by creating players so marvelous to watch fans will pack stadiums to cheer them on. Where Derek was in the summer of 1992 was a long way from this fulfillment.

Minor-league teams are where everyone starts and no one hopes to stay. The Kalamazoo youngster would be playing with (and against) boys just like him, hoping to realize their big-league dreams quickly and successfully.

He would also be up against players of several seasons who hadn't yet performed well enough to get into the big leagues, and who were facing the growing threats of time and indifference from their managers. In addition, injured major-league players frequently wind up being sent back to do time in the minors. Placed on the disabled list, hurt headliners can prove their return to health with less risk to the big team (and, usually, less media attention) by successfully playing a few minor league games. Such players are always eager to show their bosses they have recovered from whatever injury benched them and that they are ready to rejoin their clubs. (Jeter himself would be in this position a few years later.) And there are veteran major leaguers in the minors, too, men who've lost their spark due to injury or overwork, or simply have not managed to perform to original expectations. A minor-league position gives them one more chance to prove they are worth the time and money and attention due bona-fide baseball stars.

All of this was a lot to come up against; but Jeter was no doubt wide-eyed and excited as he arrived in Tampa, Florida to play for the Gulf Coast Rookie League. He must have felt ready and eager to throw, catch, run, and swing his way right into the New York Yankees.

Actually, his first game as a professional baseball player didn't go very well. He first stepped up to the plate no doubt brimming with excitement. He finished the doubleheader 0-7, no doubt considerably less excited.

"What Derek does in his first few games isn't that important when you look at the career we think he'll have with us," Mitch Luikevics, the director of minor-league Yankee operations, said. This was welcome news, because Derek continued not to perform well— beyond the first few games. Practically the entire season was a comedown for the whiz from Kalamazoo.

Even a natural has a lot to learn and Jeter's success, as we have seen, was a mixture of natural ability; hard, hard work; massive amounts of encouragement and support; and the crucial element no one can guess at or master—luck. Nobody's success lasts forever. Ability in even the most gifted athlete doesn't advance in a steady course. The rush to a full-time career has to catch up with a beginner sometime, and this is when it caught up to Derek Jeter.

He was a brilliant young athlete, sure. But he was also an 18-year-old, on his own and playing as a professional for the first time. And, he was arriving in Tampa amid great anticipation—the Yankees' number-one draft pick, the sixth overall, even though he was barely out of high school. Everyone must have been watching him with excitement and demands and intensity, and Derek himself, putting on (minor-league) Yankee togs, must have thought he'd died and gone to baseball heaven.

What they saw on the Tampa ball fields was a first season that was not up to expectations. Jeter's performance was not brilliant. Some have called it an outright disaster—stretching things, maybe.

What on earth happened? After so many years and so much work (and so much success) how could this have happened? Several possibilities suggest themselves. . . .

Baseball heaven? Not exactly . . . The Yankees have a four-stadium complex in Tampa, where their main offices are and players from all levels of the Yankee organization train and perform. Tampa, Florida, in summertime is rough. Early in the morning, it gets hot. And even worse is the humidity—while Kalamazoo might have a humid spell now and then, muggy weather is the norm in Tampa. Walking for more than a few minutes can leave a person saturated and breathless. And the Tampa Gulf Coasters were doing baseball morning, noon, and, sometimes, nights.

The work to be done was considerable, and the schedule rough. Mornings were for practice. Games would sometimes be played in the afternoons, but schedules were often subject to change. On a given morning, Derek could hurry out of bed to the sports complex and not be sure of what he would have to do that day. Changing the schedule was not a big deal, because these games do not even remotely resemble big-league competitions: They aren't public events wherein the players receive the encouragement of a stadium full of rabid watchers. Spectators were seldom seen at the A-level games, no doubt to force the players to focus completely on their baseball skills and not worry about (or play to) the crowds.

In other words, Derek Jeter went from performing exceptionally well in his hometown in front of supportive, even adoring, colleagues and spectators to toiling in miserable weather through silent games surrounded by empty bleachers, having to deal with all of this and his own inner fears alone. He didn't have a car, and most other forms of amusement (if he still, at this point, considered baseball an amusement) were some distance, which meant his life consisted of baseball, meals, TV, and what solace he could get on the telephone. Instead of wafting up to baseball heaven, the kid must have felt he'd crash-landed into minor-league purgatory.

At one game, during Jeter's first weeks of professional play, reporter Paul Morgan, who had incisively (perhaps hopefully) inscribed Derek Jeter's boyhood promise into the journalistic record, arrived in Tampa to see how his big new career was going. Well. Morgan and 11 other spectators sweltered as they watched two beginner teams lurch through a game. Occasionally, he noted Yankee managerial personnel wandering in, watching a bit of the game, then wandering out. Morgan kept coming up with the word *strange*.

He talked to Derek—"You don't have much time to do much else except play ball," he commented, perhaps sounding a bit numb. He talked to Yankee brass, perhaps bracing himself for what they could possibly say about the local hero, but they expressed enthusiasm for Derek's performance, telling Morgan to let the Kalamazooans know the favorite son was doing fine. The team manager, Gary Denbo, backed them up. "There are a lot of things Derek does that we like."

Like *what*? Morgan must have thought. Batting .210? Making more errors in a few games than he'd probably thought Derek could make in an entire season? Morgan did realize they're called *minor* leagues for a reason. The Yankee scout had reported faithfully on Derek's abilities, and his new owners knew from experience that if he wasn't performing now, odds were with time and adjustments he would.

Still, Morgan's report to his readers not long after wasn't a sparkling one. It was titled "Few cheers in rookie league."

HEELLLP! . . . Prior to this inaugural pro season, Derek Jeter had never been away from his parents for more than a few days at a time, usually while traveling with the Kalamazoo Maroons. A photograph taken about the time of his draft by the Yankees, seen in the light of where he was now, is heartbreaking; Dot and Charles Jeter are on the left, beaming at both their children: Sharlee is hoisted up in the air by her father and, at the edge of the picture, her brother. Everyone is smiling (Sharlee right into the camera with a winning, familiar grin), but Derek looks a little less happy. In fact, he looks incredibly young and small . . . like his future's just tripped and fallen on him.

With nobody in the stands to cheer him on, with strangers for teammates and managers, with overheated-looking men in shirts and ties watching him play, and with no family to come home to, it's not much of a wonder that Derek was making a rough adjustment.

He didn't exactly keep it to himself.

"I called home *all* the time," he admitted later. And he apparently had a lot to talk about.

A pattern formed back in Kalamazoo, and it lasted well into Jeter's 1993 playing season. Late at night in the Jeter residence, the phone would ring. The Jeters would look at each other. As later recalled to *Bergen Record* reporter Rafael Hermoso, Dr. Jeter would turn to Mrs. Jeter and say, "Mom, you take this one." (At least they took turns.) The parent of the night would go to the phone, listening sympathetically to the tired son's latest defeats, problems, anxieties, and pangs of homesickness.

"I was making errors every day," Derek remembered, no doubt not happily. "I was saying, 'Maybe they won't hit another ground ball to shortstop,' and it was only the first two weeks of the season."

After comforting their son, the Jeters would discuss what went wrong with his playing, and suggest means of correction. They also urged him to not hold on to his mistakes. Charles Jeter has said this was a problem with his own baseball playing, and he was concerned his son would demonstrate similar tendencies. (This became one of the best lessons Derek received in these early years.) After everything their son had been through, it was clear his family wasn't about to let him flinch and run at the first obstacle in his career.

Even if it meant tripping over himself on the ball field.

"I was trying to figure it out and I couldn't," Derek later explained, and he found himself thinking that perhaps college was where he should be. Perhaps he didn't always like the family's adamant "Stick with it!" and "Keep swinging!" He kept calling, though, and the advice didn't change, so he must have agreed with it and wanted to hear it again on some level.

His loneliness wasn't surprising. He had gone through a thrilling, but also staggering, number of changes in his life in a few months. Baseball had always been his life; now he was discovering what it was like to have *only* baseball in your life. The other elements of existence that had been there for him in Kalamazoo— his friends, teachers, school, girlfriends, the entire community that surrounded him—were thousands of miles away. When you are in a new phase of life, thinking about the old one (and wondering why you left it) can get very tough.

And what game is this? . . . Derek Jeter was prized in Kalamazoo, among other reasons, for his 80-mile-an-hour-plus throws. In Tampa, he was batting against pitchers capable of whizzing balls in his direction well over *90* miles an hour. He had never played against so many people who were as good—or better, even *a lot* better—than he was.

Prior to this summer, he had faced only a few knuckleball pitches, and some of them were probably accidental knuckle balls, at that. The ones he started getting hurled at him in Tampa weren't, but he kept going.

For the first month of minor league, the Yankees change little in their players' games. They want to spend time just watching the newcomers, seeing how they manage over time, what long- and short-range changes are needed in performance, and how they will go about making them. Once those 30 days are over, however, the long, hard work of turning promise into professionalism begins in earnest.

They could see what they had was special, despite the obvious goofs and uncertainties. Eventually, Derek did get a hit—in the first game of a double-header. Not much of a hit, but it led to more in the second game that day. (Imagine how ecstatic *that* night's call home must have been!)

And despite fumbling, falling, and, occasionally,

looking as if he just discovered he had feet, his natural abilities (the speedy hands and feet, the hair-trigger reflexes, the powerful arm) and acquired skills (the thorough knowledge of baseball, the complete commitment to it) were showing through, too.

For starters, Jeter was put on a weight training program. He arrived in Tampa a skinny fellow, 6'2" and 162 pounds.* What he needed, right away, was more of himself. Weight training was a recent adoption of major league baseball teams; for a long time, pumping iron was thought to slow players down. (Bear in mind that in 1992 the shattering of Babe Ruth's and Roger Maris's home-run records by the brawny power-lifting devotee Mark McGwire was six seasons in the future.) But, as players began lifting weights and taking supplements themselves, the results, especially for those expected to be heavy hitters, were obvious. Derek benefited from this enlightened approach to weight training, and has continued to get bigger and stronger throughout his first Yankee seasons, eventually topping 185 pounds.

Derek also received the kind of basic, day-in, day-out baseball coaching that can be priceless to a potential major leaguer. When you come in each morning and are expected to do nothing but hit the ball, over and over again, for a few hours, then run through one or two defensive plays again and again, then have lunch, then come back and play a nine-inning game with the fresh experience of the morning's work still in your muscles and memory, you can't help but become a sharper, better player, unless the whole thing just wears you out. It wouldn't have been surprising if it hadn't—in just over two months, Jeter and his teammates played 60 games.

*Accounts of Jeter's height at this period cite both 6'2" and 6'3" (his current statistic). As he was still a teenager, he may have continued to grow in this year, explaining the discrepancy.

But it wasn't. Derek was an excellent student, the kind of player who seeks advice and learns from it quickly. Jeter profiles are full of such testimonials, whether from his Tampa coach, Mike Arena, or Willie Randolph and Joe Torre of the Yankees—Jeter even welcomes notes from his teammates.

This summer, Arena told Paul Morgan (making yet another trip to watch Derek the pro) he was impressed on several counts. "There have been some plays he's made that I didn't think he would get to," Arena noted. "He's gone into the hole and put the throw right on the dime."

Visits from his family certainly helped. (On at least one occasion the Jeters were flown to Tampa by Yankee management.) Jeter also received a visit from his Kalamazoo girlfriend. Unfortunately, he was too busy practicing and playing to do much with his visitors.

By the end of August, the young athlete's first season in the minors was almost done. He played 11 games for the Yankees' minors team in Greensboro, North Carolina (he would return to that team next year). And, at the very end, there was a treat: The Yankees brought him to New York for a weekend in September to see the stadium and meet his pro colleagues. That must have been the perfect end to a grueling season, and a reminder of what all his hard work was for. Once that was done, Derek returned to Kalamazoo, rested, probably reveled in the cooler weather, and prepared for his first semester studying at Western Michigan University.

It's important not to make too much of this difficult first season in the minors, though. Reading descriptions of what was going wrong, it sounds, in retrospect, difficult but not hopeless. Jeter was making errors, and his batting average, which had been .557 in his record-shattering junior year at Kalamazoo Central, dwindled to a humiliating .202 in Tampa. The greater demands of professional baseball—the faster pace, the greater skills needed for batting and fielding—were a lot for a beginner to assimilate. In hindsight, it's not surprising that he met the initial challenges in Tampa by tripping up on the field.

Jeter himself supports this view. ''I was trying to figure it out and I couldn't,'' he told a reporter. ''I began thinking, maybe I should have gone to school.''

''He went through a lot of struggles,'' Don Zomer, his coach back in Kalamazoo, says. ''He had a lot of errors, was throwing the ball all over the place. Even Derek himself would sometimes say the Yanks wasted their money on him. But that's another thing about Derek—we would talk about having the tools, but he also has the desire to be the *best*.''

Back home, he still got the best possible advice from his parents: ''Stick to it.'' It must have been tempting for all the Jeters to consider that Derek at least had alternatives. If he was simply too lonely and confused to continue with the Yankees' A team in Tampa, he could always accept the position on the baseball team that had been offered him from the University of Michigan. (The Jeters, remember, had insisted the Yankees pay for his education at Michigan.) And, if this didn't work out, he could always stay home and figure out his next move.

But ''Stick to it'' was really the only answer for a player of Derek's potential and ambitions. He was already part of the Yankees, just a few teams away from his lifetime goal, the *New York* Yankees. It would have been foolish, at this point, to give up. So, he hung in there, and gradually, but persistently, began to get his bearings, and get better. Soon he would be astonishing them in the minor leagues.

His first season in the minors concluded, he did the fall semester at the University of Michigan, studying business administration. Then, early in 1993 he spent his first full season at Greensboro, North Carolina, in the South Atlantic league. This is when something happened to Derek Jeter, for his game picked up considerably.

What was it? He has given a single-word answer: "Confidence."

If a person finds one level of achievement intimidating, it is safe to assume a higher level will appear even more formidable. This is exactly what did *not* happen to Jeter. At Greensboro, he reported for spring training and was surrounded by professionals with greater experience than he. Rather than being cowed by this, he responded well, and began observing how his longstanding colleagues worked.

"I saw how the big league players carried themselves," he's explained. "I saw how they went about their work." These were men who lived and breathed baseball, as he had always wanted to do. Their calm, constant ability, how they encountered and solved problems on the field, were all instructive to the younger player.

Jeter also made an important discovery: What separated the veterans from beginners like himself was, more than anything else, something he had already sensed was of primary importance for a professional sports career: consistency, not just higher ability, of performance. They were better at what they did than a rookie with a lot to learn, of course. What really mattered, though, was how securely they relied on their bodies, their senses, their reactions, to function capably on the ballfield. Erratic performances are to be taken for granted in a beginner. Now, Jeter was eager to become as consistent and professional as his more experienced teammates.

If you study the shortstop exclusively throughout a game, keeping an eye on him even when he is not in play, you quickly notice that Derek is a great *watcher*. There's hardly a moment of baseball time when he seems bored, distracted, or running alternative fantasies through his head. For the three or four hours of a game, he is a 100 percent participant in every second of action. Even on the bench, even on the bench after a strikeout, he doesn't sink into himself or stalk about like other players do: He grabs a cup of water, maybe wordlessly apologizing to Joe Torre with a slight shake of his head (and Torre's eyes flash reprimands faster and better than anyone in baseball), and then sits down to watch the game, as eager as any benchwarmer in the bleachers. ("He watches just like *us*," a young Jeter fan complimented during the 1998 World Series.)

It helps when you have people better at your sport to watch, too. At Greensboro, Jeter was mixing with players of all kinds, unlike just the beginners in Tampa. Mundane things helped: It's cooler in Greensboro. And having gained several pounds of muscle thanks to weight-training in the off-season, Jeter was not only older, but stronger. Confidence got an additional boost when he spent part of spring training with the New York Yankees.

"It's interesting to see how things work on the major-league level," Derek said earnestly to a reporter from the *Sun-Sentinel* of Fort Lauderdale. (Reporters, usually allergic to earnest enthusiasm, seem charmed to the core by Derek.) "You learn about the great players, and when you get around them, you see the game is the same." And then he added: "Being here will help me feel more comfortable next time. I didn't know how much I'd play, but how much I play isn't really important."

Next time. Confidence was mutating into certainty. The kid baseball fanatic had taken a beating last season. Now the grown up, professional athlete was ready to emerge.

This is precisely what happened to Derek at Greensboro in 1993. He began to play better, more firmly. He became more and more of a professional and, once again, acute observers began mentioning how he played baseball with a wisdom and skill far beyond his years. (This statement seems to have been made by at least one observer at every period of Jeter's baseball life. The same has been said for other precocious sportsmen—the preteen Tiger Woods was a fine example.)

At the end of the 1993 season in Greensboro, Jeter's confidence was considerably justified. After playing 128 games and 515 at-bats, he earned a batting average of .295, making 14 doubles, 11 triples, five home runs, and 71 RBIs. His confidence also fueled his sense of daring again: Jeter stole 18 bases. Anyone who's seen Jeter play for the Yankees knows that stealing bases is an activity he appears to live for: one part of him seems to be always, *always*, looking to steal. When he does, he seems to charge not from one base to another but dash through the air six inches above the playing field, his limbs somehow extending themselves, his arms pumping sky, as if with the next burst of energy he would bound not just around the baseball diamond but clear out of the stadium. This gleeful daring inflames the whole stadium at times, especially enchanting Jeter watchers. There were already plenty of those in the minor leagues—in fact, the league voted Derek its prospect of the year.

He had done so well, actually, that Jeter hoped to move beyond Greensboro, to the next, closer step to the Yankees. The Yankees have a AA affiliate team in the Eastern League in Albany, New York. It wasn't the Yankees' top minor-league team (that was in Columbus, Ohio) but the move to Albany would have brought Derek tantalizingly close to *the* House, Yankee Stadium in the Bronx. Not yet twenty, he was clearly hoping for a lot. But with the rising tide of talent and achievement announcing itself in game after game, who could blame him?

And who could blame him for being disappointed when the new assignment came from the Yanks—and it wasn't up north to Albany but south, again, to Tampa, where he had had such a hard first season?

Even when thwarted, Jeter's response is moderate. "I was upset when they told me," he admitted to a reporter. "You ask anyone and they'll tell you they'd like to get there [into the big leagues] as soon as possible. But I got over it."

He demonstrated here the same philosophical acceptance of whatever comes, as any fan can see at work when Derek steps up to the plate for the Yanks and things don't go well. Jeter doesn't appear to agonize over mistakes; he has a constant ability to put things in perspective. After losses, he is the player reporters flock to for a considered, healing comment (David Cone is another), a promise that it's not the end of the world and the next game will be better. (When the Yankees suffered a punishing loss to the Cleveland Indians in the '98 pennant race, TV news reports showed Jeter musing frankly on the defeat and on the chance to make up for it in the next game. This was expected: What wasn't was the pullback shot of a ring of seasoned reporters, clearly shaken by the loss, listening hopefully to Derek's words.) This consoling clearheadedness is not a quality common to players of major-league baseball, least of all in the heat of competition. When plays are missed or strikeouts called, tempers flare, bats are dropped or hurled or even broken, gloves are slammed to the ground in despair. Baseball is a matter of life and death to players and fans, but the players who *live* those life-and-death moments take their defeats most bitterly.

Part of being a devotee is hanging in there with your favorite when the chips are down, but, sometimes, favorites don't make it easy. Some Yankee fans dread Paul O'Neill striking out, or David Cone watching a batter send one over the fence. O'Neill will give himself a mental drubbing when he screws up, stalking away muttering with such a tight face it hurts to watch. ("Will you *relax*, for God's sake?!" a frustrated fan once screamed at O'Neill as he trotted off to the dugout miserably.) When a ball he has just pitched sails over his head for a run, Cone suddenly resembles a frightened child helpless before the disapproval of 57,000 parents. And there can be no more disturbing sight in Yankee Stadium—even that of George Steinbrenner—than when a game takes a turn for the worse, and the eyes of Joe Torre darken with suspicion, and his face armors itself as if against an armada of defeat. (And imagine what the player who screwed up feels as he approaches to explain himself to that face!) But Jeter, when he misses a ball or is caught out, shrugs, shakes his head, sometimes smiles ruefully. Then it's gone. Very rarely will you notice him reacting gravely, as he did in Game 2 of the 1998 World Series—after striking out a second time, he exited visibly put out, eyes somber, walk tight with frustration. Even this unusual response didn't last: Minutes later, he was alert and focused again, happiest of men in baseball. (Besides, as a Jeter admirer puts it, "He's cute even when he goofs.")

This ability to let go of rancor over mistakes can be priceless to an athlete. They must make peace with failure quickly, for the best of them fail again and again. Even Babe Ruth and Joe DiMaggio and Mickey Mantle, three absolutely immortal Yankees, did time at bat striking out. So when Jeter didn't get the rotation news he'd hoped for, he accepted and made the best of it. He has said he understands there are things in his career he can't command, and knows worrying about those things won't help any. In other words, the lesson he learned that day many years ago from his Dad—don't blame others; control what you can control—really has proved as crucial as it sounded that day.

Besides, he must have known, somewhere, that returning to Tampa was not a serious setback but another opportunity to prove himself.

The weeks back in Florida proved to be exceptional. Derek reported early in 1994 to the Class A Florida League in Tampa and almost immediately showed himself far, far more ready for the big leagues than his age and experience suggested. In the short time he was there, he hit a wallopingly better .329 in 292 at-bats, with 96 singles, 13 doubles, eight triples. He batted in 39 runs, and stole 28 bases. He didn't have to wait much longer to get to Albany—in June of 1994, he was promoted there.

Derek didn't even stay in Albany very long. He performed so well, and seemed so filled with confidence and accomplishment, that the Yankee managers quickly zipped him to the last minors club they had left to promote him to—the Class AAA Columbus Clippers in the International League. As it happened, the promotion came on the same day as the deadline for trading in the major leagues. When Derek was told to report to the Albany manager's office, he hesitated—had he been traded? An onlooker can stare at this reaction in amazement: Traded? With the season he was having? However, there was some logic to it. The Yankees had been notorious for using their minor leaguers as trading chips for already-established major-leaguers (I'll trade you three talented minors for one star, for example). In so doing, they gained some fine professionals and lost some beginners who would grow into even finer professionals. The front office's holding onto Derek was part of a new commitment to Yankee young people that in just a few seasons would bear fruit.

In Columbus, he continued to flourish, and it became

clear that Derek Jeter, although not quite 20 years old, was too old and wise a player for the minor leagues. "The kid has come in and looked like he belonged from the day he got here," the Clippers manager, Stump Merrill, told the Associated Press.

Jeter played 35 games with Columbus in 1994, hitting three homers and 16 RBIs. (His batting average was .349.) He hit in 28 of 35 games for the Clippers.

Unfortunately, problems beyond Jeter's control— way, *way* beyond Jeter's control—were affecting his future, and possibly the future of baseball itself.

It was so obvious that Derek Jeter was a baseball player of enormous potential that he started getting the attention of fans, press, and Yankee management big time in 1994. There were rumors of a sudden promotion to the major leagues. Hearing them, Derek kept cool. This turned out, in hindsight, to be wise, because around the time a decision should have been made, the sport he had dedicated his life to floundered, fell, and stopped dead in its tracks.

Of all the ruinous effects of the 1994 major-league baseball strike, one of the least devastating was on Derek Jeter's career. He didn't make it to the Yankees in 1994, but he continued to play for the Columbus Clippers. New Yorkers were so starved for baseball that a Clippers game was broadcast to the metropolitan area—giving New Yorkers their first live glimpse of the shortstop they were soon to know big-time.

However, the strike was disturbing to the teams, the managers, their fans, and the whole public. There was an awful sense that a century of tradition and triumph was being wasted via squabbling between players and management. Resentment solidified. And, when it became clear there wasn't going to be a 1994 World Series and October would be just another month of football, resentment escalated to something worse—indifference.

For hardcore fans it was like enduring a death in the family. That October, PBS broadcast a nine-part, 18-hour television series, *Baseball*, produced by Ken Burns, that had been carefully timed to premiere before the World Series, when baseball fever always reaches its height. Instead, this brilliantly produced, eloquent tribute to America's sport fell on hurt, frustrated ears, seeming like, at best, bad timing, and at worst, a cruel joke. "If it was meant to be a celebration, it felt more like a funeral," one viewer remarked. When cynicism overtakes baseball fans, you know something dangerous is occurring.

The worst didn't come to pass. Eventually, the strike was settled. Just before, managements began recruiting replacement players, in case the '95 season looked to be a washout, too. Derek, when asked if he would ever be a replacement player, issued a firm "Never. The players are striking for something which is [for] our benefit." And then he added, showing a sharp eye he doesn't often demonstrate in public: "You'd have an 'X' on your back for the rest of your career if you did that. I can see maybe older players who have been at Triple A for awhile and haven't had their shot yet maybe becoming replacements, but I don't think enough players will want to do it."

On another level, though, Derek Jeter was shaping up into an antidote to the strike. With no playoffs or World Series to write about, sports watchers took gratefully to the minor leagues, where Jeter was winning awards and arousing enthusiasm. On September 14, 1994, during a ceremony at Yankee Stadium, he was named *Baseball America*'s Minor League Player of the Year. (The same publication, remember, had honored Derek in his high school days.) He was also named to similar awards by *The Sporting News*, *Baseball Weekly*, and *Topps*.

Baseball America's managing editor, Jim Callis, was

effusive, calling Derek "One of the most exciting short-stops to come into minor league baseball in years. He excelled at three different levels in 1994, and never missed a beat in shooting from Class-A all the way to Triple-A. We are extremely confident that Derek will be another in the long line of *Baseball America* minor league players of the year who've gone on to successful careers in the major leagues." Recent winners of this award include Derek Bell, Sandy Alomar, Jr., Dwight Gooden, and Jose Canseco.

Sports writers and fans, starved for baseball—period—began studying Derek's records in amazement. Taken in one gulp, they communicate effectively the velocity of his development and the headiness of his talents.

While in Greensboro in 1992 and 1993 he played 139 games (11 during his ill-fated first season in 1992). His batting average there in 1993 was .295, with 14 doubles, 11 triples, five home runs, and 71 RBIs. The 56 errors that season were still problematic (he was the second most error-prone shortstop in his league) but, even so, he gained admiration. The excitement Jeter communicates on the field can make observers put even errors in perspective.

Then, in 1994, he zipped through the three levels of the Yankees' minor leagues, and his batting average climbed to .377 in the Albany/Eastern league, and .349 in Columbus' International league. He scored 42 runs in Albany and Columbus, making 90 hits and 13 errors. All in a few months.

He was growing in confidence, capitalizing on the increasingly effective advice he had been getting (Derek has credited his Greensboro manager, Brian Butterfield, with being especially helpful on improving his defense), and becoming a magnet for attention. Baseball admirers were already drawing on his tremendous energy.

Even the Yankees were buzzing about him. With no end-of-season theme in the present to showcase their October issue (aside from the strike), the editors of *Yankees* magazine put Derek on the cover. A portrait of the older, stronger, handsomer Columbus Clipper ran under the cover headline "The Yankees' Look Of The Future."

At this point, Derek demonstrated one of his greatest gifts: the ability to accept praise yet not have his head turned by it. Compliments from reporters would be answered by brief but sincere promises to keep working, keep concentrating. He knew consistency was still an issue, and brought it up himself—"You've got to make the plays over and over," he told the *Columbus Dispatch.*

Writers were demonstrating that Jeter was already a major-leaguer—they began comparing him to great players of the present and past. Some remembered Bucky Dent, the last star shortstop for the Yankees, but when a reporter for the *St. Louis Post-Dispatch* struck such a comparison, Derek fielded it as deftly as any grounder.

"In terms of comparing myself to anyone else, I don't do that," was his firm answer. "I try not to rate myself. I've had a pretty good year, that's true. But I've got a lot to improve on.

"I'm always working to get a little better."

Meanwhile, back in Yankeeland, management was trying to make a decision: Should they promote Derek Jeter, who was described by top Yankee personnel as "a treasure," but was still pretty much a teenager, or should they sign an experienced (if occasionally injured) veteran, Tony Fernandez? As much as Jeter's promise tantalized the Yanks (especially while staggering under the long-term effects of the strike), the decision was made to stick with experience: Fernandez signed a two-year, $3 million contract, and Jeter was given another year of seasoning and strengthening in the minors.

If things had gone this way in 1995, that would not have been so bad. Derek had only been in the minors three years, a short time. (Champion Yankees like Don Mattingly did five years or more before getting the big call.) Another season wouldn't be a setback. Besides, the Yankees clearly wanted their prospect to know they were still rooting for him—then-General Manager Gene Michael called Jeter at home after the decision was made to explain it himself. Michael, Derek told a reporter, "told me not to read anything into [the decision], to not worry about it."

So, Derek opened the 1995 season back in the minors, ready to keep working and waiting for the next step, which he knew would be coming sometime—but when? "I've still got more steps to make and the strike stopped that step last season," he reasoned. "It'll work out."

The Columbus Clippers were happy to have him: He was a brilliant player that lifted the whole team, fans were already starting to circle when Jeter played, and we know what good company the guy himself is.

However, things went wrong for the Yankees in 1995. Suddenly, Derek Jeter, minor-leaguer, was no longer a luxury they could afford.

Back in Kalamazoo on May 28, Charles and Dorothy Jeter heard their phone ring yet again. It had been two seasons since those long, painful calls from their confused, tired little boy. Perhaps they knew (the way parents often do) this was another call from their son. This time, he wasn't crying from homesickness, or frustrated from tripping over himself and scoring another error, or breathless from another evening when his learning and playing were coming together, or thrilled from another great play. This time Derek was making a call, *the* call, the one he had been dreaming and working toward with his family's help since leaving home. He was calling to tell them he had just been promoted from Class AAA Columbus to the major leagues. He'd been ordered to replace the Yankees' current shortstop, Tony Fernandez, who was injured. He would meet the team on the road and go right into play. Derek Jeter, 20 years old, was a New York Yankee.

Derek's sister Sharlee answered, heard the news, and immediately handed the phone to her father. The son put it simply: "Dad, I'm out of here." The Jeters were described as "practically doing backflips" by their equally ecstatic home paper. "It was so totally unexpected, that it was a real shock," Dr. Jeter said later. Backflips probably couldn't have begun to express their joy. This was a family that had put so much heart and soul where it belonged—in the rearing of their children—and, unlike other families that had worked just as hard, they were seeing all their hopes for their son come true faster, bigger, more gloriously, than perhaps they had ever dared to hope.

The Jeters' commitment to both their children was demonstrated by their handling of the next dilemma. Derek informed them he was on his way at once to Seattle to join the Yankees—but Sharlee, a ballplayer herself (even, like her brother, you may recall, a shortstop) was about to play an important district tournament game as part of Kalamazoo Central High School's team. If Derek needed his parents with him to make the jump to the Yanks, if his major-league debut would go infinitely easier knowing he would at least be playing before a few familiar, loving, supportive faces in the stands, his little sister needed the same assurance. Other families might have cried "But this is the *Yankees*," and urged their daughter to give up her game and accompany them to Seattle. The Jeters, however, reached a solution with typical clearsightedness: Dr. Jeter flew to Seattle to be with their son; Mrs. Jeter attended the Kalamazoo Central game, to cheer on their daughter.

There were others who rapidly heard the news—neighbors, fellow students, teachers, friends, who had watched and encouraged the young athlete, who must have been bowled over with happiness as well. When Hillary Clinton used the venerable African saying, "It takes a village to raise a child," to serve as the title of her best-selling book, the First Lady couldn't have been thinking of young Derek Jeter, at this moment hurriedly packing his bags to meet his future in Seattle, but his life, his family, and his already stunning achievement provide a good example of everything Mrs. Clinton was writing about. Time and again when studying Jeter's story, one hears or reads the words of grateful, admiring people. The very repetition of enthusiasm, of faith in this young man, can get your suspicions aroused. Then, you read them again, and realize such sincerity is real and deeply felt. The competition, envy, and carping that often surround a person capable of excellence simply don't appear around Derek Jeter. The luck he experienced on the playing field grew from the strength he had (and must still draw from) thanks to a supportive, admiring community.

Although these durable bonds of support would bring Jeter back to Kalamazoo again and again to see family and neighbors, when he would be treated by all as a favorite son, in a certain sense Derek Jeter's years in Kalamazoo had come to an end. Now, he was a citizen of a game, and a culture, and his home would be the grandest, toughest, most rewarding palace in baseball.

"Out of all of the promising young athletes to emerge from development programs, including high school and college competition, only a handful have made it to the big time," the *Kalamazoo Gazette*'s sports editor, Jack Moss, wrote in a jubilant column leading off a special section of the paper on Jeter's ascension to the major leagues. "Jeter is the first Kalamazoo product in the majors since Mike Squires retired in 1985. . . . It's almost a one-in-a-million shot for a young man or woman making it to the top in professional sports."

Moss concluded with words Derek's family must have found as stirring as the news he was finally joining the Yankees, "Whether he becomes a superstar in baseball or not, we'd bet that Jeter will eventually earn his college degree."

Bob Hertzel, at the *Bergen Record*, put it quite succinctly: "The Derek Jeter era of Yankee baseball is imminent."

Fourth Inning

Yankee

"It's great to be young and a Yankee."
— Joe DiMaggio

The newest New York Yankee's youth and energy and dashing skills were badly needed—his team was not performing well. More than his own team was ailing: The whole sport was struggling to survive after a prior season of much scandal, shock, disillusionment, and bitterness. From glowing with the innocent enthusiasm of teamwork and excellence, ''the National Pastime'' as it is called, was looking suspect, its participants greedy and cynical, even (to some) dishonest. Attendance was slumping. Players and management, normally at odds, were united in their alarm. How to win back the public's trust, earn the devotion of fans, and renew their sport? It turned out it would take a player who had no connection to the scandals of the past, a new man, one full of love for the sport and athletic power and beauty. He appeared on the scene in his new Yankee uniform, played, and immediately provoked gasps of amazement and delight from onlookers. Suddenly, the troubles of baseball mattered less than the genius of this guy who was able, with his skills and charisma, to make the sport hot and thrilling and *real* again.

No, we're not in 1995—it's 1920, and the player is

George Herman Ruth, soon to be known by the whole world as "Babe," or "the Bambino." As fine a player as Derek Jeter is, he doesn't quite measure up to the phenomenon of Babe Ruth, who was not so much a baseball player as a force of nature sporting a Yankee uniform. But the rapture he caused, the sense that his sheer love for and brilliance at the game would go a long way to redeeming it, sends eerie echoes through Derek Jeter's story—especially at this moment, with the young minor leaguer on the verge of joining the team Ruth helped make the standard in baseball.

The 1919 Chicago White Sox were thought to be the greatest club ever assembled. Led by slugger Shoeless Joe Jackson and ace hurler Eddie Cicotte, they were the favorites to beat the National League's Cincinnati Reds in the World Series. However, the first two games were marred by uncharacteristically sloppy fielding and pitching by the White Sox (also known as the Pale Hose). The word was everywhere that the Series had been fixed—lost by the White Sox deliberately. The Reds won the Fall Classic, five games to four, leaving a confused and disillusioned nation angry and disappointed.

The following year, eight members of the White Sox were charged with conspiring with gamblers to throw the Series. Included among the accused were Jackson and Cicotte, along with Chick Gandil, the player who was the contact with the gamblers. Nobody went to jail for throwing the series, but Judge Kenesaw Mountain Landis, baseball's first commissioner, banned them from the game for life. The whole baseball culture shuddered dangerously over "the astounding and contemptible crime of selling out the baseball world," as *The Sporting News* put it. The eight men out, the paper continued, "will be remembered from now on only for the depths of depravity to which they could sink."

What saved baseball from sinking into the same muck

was the unsurpassed genius for the game of Babe Ruth, and the charm with which he appeared before a public disillusioned by the scandal and shaken still more from the carnage of the First World War and the convulsive social changes that sped through Roaring Twenties. Babe Ruth rescued baseball, initiating what became known as the Golden Age of Sport, in which his own virtuoso playing vied for public attention with such sports gods as Jack Dempsey (boxing), Red Grange (football), Big Bill Tilden (tennis), and Man o' War (thoroughbred racing). Ruth was not alone: he helped his team initiate their still-unrivalled record of trips to the World Series (in 1995, the Yankees had won 22 World Series titles and competed in a total of 33 World Series competitions). And Ruth insured baseball's long-term survival, his own excellence setting off chain-reactions of ideals and accomplishments in other pro ballparks and countless baseball clubs, sandlots, and city streets across America for two generations.

Derek Jeter was joining the New York Yankees right after the draining, even humiliating, 1994 season, which was filled with disagreements and warnings, and finally screeched to a dead halt (just as his own Yankee future seemed to) with the baseball strike. The Yankees do have an amazing history, but they weren't living up to it in 1995. Their last World Series win had been in 1978. Their owner, George Steinbrenner III, one of the most colorful, recognized, and infamous public figures in New York, was becoming more talked about than his team, for his outspoken behavior and firing and trading sprees. (One Yankee observer joked the various ex-managers and coaches and players George had fired were so numerous they were eligible to form their own union.) The team was in immediate trouble, too, as *both* their short-stop (Tony Fernandez) and second baseman (Pat Kelly) were suddenly on the disabled list. Fernandez had strained a ribcage muscle, and hoped to be ready to play in early June. Kelly's injury was worse—a damaged ligament in his left wrist due to a checked swing. So, if Derek Jeter always wanted to be a Yankee, right now the Yankees just plain needed Derek Jeter.

He joined the team and, immediately, the freshness, dedication, and complete immersion in baseball that teammates, coaches, relatives, and early observers had been exclaiming over for 20 years became clear to the wider circle that follows every Yankee move. In 1995, Derek didn't save the Yankees, or the sport, but he certainly gave both a drastically needed breath of youth, and a glimpse of their (and his) future.

First, Derek had a plane to catch to Seattle, where the Yanks were beginning a three-game visit fighting the Mariners. They had just lost a game to the Oakland A's, managing one hit but no score. They had lost nine of their last eleven games. So far that season, their wins totaled an even dozen—and their losses, 14. *Bergen Record* sports writer Bob Hertzel was merciless but accurate assessing the team Derek Jeter was eagerly joining: "If it weren't for bad news the Yankees would be making no news at all."

After seven hours in the air, Derek arrived in Seattle and immediately prepared for his debut as a New York Yankee. It was a rushed beginning, but not a completely cold one: He had joined the team at spring training, and become familiar with players and management. Besides, considering what the Yankees were going through, manager Buck Showalter must have greeted this excited rookie with relief. (No injuries! No superagents in tow!)

Fortunately, Dr. Jeter had arrived to witness his son's promotion from minors to majors. On the surface, Derek probably didn't look much different than when father and son had last seen each other. And, in some respects, the relationship played out as usual: After the game they searched for a place to eat and talk, finding only a McDonald's open. "I treated," Dr. Jeter said.

But, at the moment on May 29, 1995 when the son became a major leaguer, wearing his new pinstriped uniform with the "2" clearly visible, it was another step of Derek's dream into the world. He was the ninth batter in the Yankee lineup which, under the circumstances, wasn't that surprising. (He would soon rise to second in the order, once he established himself as a hitter.) The fact that he didn't get a hit—he went 0-5 that day—and that the Yankees, after 12 long innings, lost to the Mariners, 8-7, didn't hurt the wonder of it. And the game wasn't a washout for him; he did well on defense that day. Getting through it was achievement enough. Now, his real life, the one he'd carefully prepared for 14 years, would begin.

Others sensed something momentous in the quiet debut. Reporting on the game, Bob Hertzel, who was to become a perceptive Jeter observer, commented, "And so began the major league career of one of the most highly touted Yankees prospects to arrive in the big leagues since Thurman Munson—and, at 20, the youngest since Jose Rijo."

Hertzel also voiced what the player and his family and friends were also wondering: Was he now with the team merely as a stopgap until injured Yankees were off the disabled list (in addition to Fernandez and Kelly, four other players were hurt), or was he at the threshold of the "career with limitless potential" he had worked for and observers were already anticipating?

"We'll address that when the time comes," responded manager Showalter. "If [Derek] is here, he will play."

Derek did what he had to—concentrated, worked, and made hopeful sounds: "All I can do is play hard and do the best I can. They're just not going to give someone the shortstop job. You can go crazy trying to think about what might happen.''

Another reporter complimented Jeter for not seeming the rookie, handling the debut with the calm of a veteran, at which Derek laughed, ''Veteran? I've got to get a hit first.''

Then, in his second game against Seattle he made the first of his dramatic major league appearances.

He didn't start out well that night—Mariners pitcher Tim Belcher struck the rookie out in the second inning with two fastballs and a slider. When he returned to bat again, however, he hit a single and was later driven in by Jim Leyritz's double, Jeter dashing across home plate to score for the first time in his major-league career.

By the seventh inning, according to Tom Friend of the *New York Times News Service*, ''the rookie was strutting. He slashes another single, this time to center, and scored his second run on [Paul] O'Neill's single, tying the score, 2-2.''

The Yankees still lost, 7-3, but Jeter had reason to be excited. Friend, summing up the enthusiasm the new shortstop was already arousing, crowed, ''It seemed he would not be leaving for Class AAA Columbus anytime soon.''

Actually, he was back in the minors three weeks later.

It wasn't that Derek didn't live up the Yankees' expectations. He was watched keenly and enthusiastically by management, but they weren't sure what to do. If Tony Fernandez returned, could they move Jeter from shortstop to second base? He had the ability, sure, but to do that to a rookie the firm had spent three years carefully developing? They felt Derek was already holding a full hand as it was.

But, before that, he played his first game at Yankee Stadium.

''Nature is a Haunted House/But Art—a house that

tries to be haunted,'' wrote Emily Dickinson, who apparently never saw a baseball game, in 1876. What she claims for art is true for that sport as well, and never more true than when you play in Yankee Stadium.

In 1998, as Derek Jeter won his second World Series, Yankee Stadium was honored for 75 years of service to players and fans. Since 1923, ''The House That Ruth Built'' had been the ultimate place to play the sport, a grand location haunted by a history no other team could lay claim to. When Derek would later get his own locker, it was next to one once occupied by (and later commemorated in his honor) Thurman Munson, a champion of Derek's childhood, whose tragic death in a 1979 plane crash stunned players and public. This locker room had been graced by many of the finest players the sport has had to offer. Home runs sailing through the air out of the yard leave in their wake a small area behind the outfield called Monument Park, a silent space filled with plaques dedicated to Ruth, Gehrig, Mantle, and other Yankee greats.

Even in the thick of competition, the awe and challenge of the Yankee standard and history haunt some of its present day practitioners. To Derek Jeter, this was living history, maybe even family history. He *understood* what motivated players to the hard work that made such achievements possible, and he had felt the same urge to excel, to reach that legendary Yankee standard.

We've followed him through his student years on the ballfield, surveyed his statistics. Before he plays his first game in Yankee Stadium, let's examine what kind of athlete is about to appear.

First of all, his understanding of what makes for a good ballplayer—the ability to seize the momentum of a play or inning or game with a strong, quick body— was thorough. Certainly, his parents and coaches helped deepen that understanding but, when watching Jeter, you sense far more than a learned behavior occurring as he hits, catches, or throws a given baseball.

After understanding comes ability. Just performing well within the context of the Little League or high-school or minor-league team he happened to be on wasn't enough of an achievement for him. One of his coaches said "He was always ahead of the other players," and almost every other coach or manager he has had echoes this claim, citing Jeter's "maturity," "awareness," "professionalism." It's not just that Jeter was a quicker study than his teammates: He saw more possible in his baseball life, from a very early age, and as fast as his body could develop to meet that possibility, he has gone after it. Never is there any sense in Jeter's behavior of someone looking for a rest, someone able to savor the awards and honors he already has and take a break. He seems to be after something bigger, a perfection of playing, an ideal game in which every sensation, reaction, move, decision, action he makes works together to create an ideal moment.

The best word to describe this striving is *inspiration*. A few commentators, sensing this aspect in the player, have likened him to a dancer, and it is true that his movements have an edge of grace and beauty you don't often see in baseball players. (One Jeter fan recently said he was "even handsomer" to watch on the ballfield than off.) It's the inspiration that causes this, the struggle to create something perfect out of a baseball game.

This is not an ideal isolated to Jeter. Early in the 1998 season, Yankee pitcher David Wells pitched a perfect game, and the team, their fans, and the entire sports world were electrified by the feat. Two seasons earlier, another Yankee pitcher, David Cone, returned from an operation for an aneurysm in his arm that many feared would destroy his career—and, in his first game, pitched a perfect seven innings. Many of baseball's most memorable moments center around such wondrous acts, and most of the sport's players have some sort of goal leading them. The best players spend their careers in a chase they know they will almost certainly never, ever win—but it's the chase that matters. Having the guts and talent to *make* that chase is the ultimate victory.

Derek Jeter just has a purity of effort and belief in him that, from the first, people recognized and responded to very powerfully. More than the youth, the looks, the charm, the early success, it's this belief that has drawn so many to him—and motivated him to perform at such a high level.

His commitment to the action of each game extends to his teammates. In grammar school, remember, he was the kid who would help other classmates with a lesson, never looking superior; he just knew what had to be done and helped others know it. You can see this same part of his character at work during the most stress-ridden, high-stakes games. Derek is the one who isn't frowning when the players talk strategy on the pitcher's mound: He listens carefully, speaks briefly and precisely, bears a confidence other players seem to take pieces of as they go back to their positions and the game begins again. He loves to win, but he loves the game a lot more. It's as if, when he was learning the history of the Yankees, it was the beauty of baseball that attracted him the most, not the triumphs available to its finest players.

Jeter also, despite his considerable gifts, never loses sight of how far he is from his goal. He is an energetic player, but sometimes overeager. He would still rather swing at a ball than just stand and draw a walk. He was taller than usual for his position, and sometimes his longer legs and arms and bigger feet would get in his way while he attempted the swift, compact saves that are part of the shortstop's job. As he progressed through his Yankee career, some of his saves—literally hurling himself into the air, over players, to get the ball—while dazzling to watch and always received with a roar of approval by crowds, were criticized as being *too* athletic. "He won't be able to do that when he's a little older," some observers complained. "He should learn how to save without jumping *now*." (Some aging shortstops wind up moving to third base.) This misses the point. Not to do the most with his mind and body just wouldn't make sense to a talent like Jeter's. He already knows how to do smaller, calmer moves and, when necessary, he certainly does them. It remained to be seen what the maturity of such a player who gains so much from youthful energy and quickness would reveal: Would he have acquired enough skills by then to make up for aging?

If Derek is, as some have said, a "baseball genius," it's in the marriage of skills with that vision of the game that makes him so. There are players who are just as accomplished technically and conscientious professionally; he isn't even the very best shortstop playing in the major leagues today, but none of those other players has exactly what Jeter has. The fusion of commitment and achievement give him an aura that, to many, is irresistible. He doesn't just play baseball, he lives and breathes it; so there was no home more perfect for his skills and dreams than Yankee Stadium, this place he instantly knew (as a little boy of six) he *must* be a part of someday.

And now he was. He went out into the stadium before the game, looked around the place while standing in the middle of the field and asked himself, "Am I really here?"

High school coach Don Zomer had promised Derek that when he played his first game as a Yankee, he would be there. "No matter where, no matter when." So, as the Yankees took to the field to warm up for

Derek's first home game in the Stadium, Zomer and Sharlee Jeter, fresh from her own victory in the Kalamazoo Central game she played the day of her brother's Yankee debut, and an old Kalamazoo friend, Josh Ewbank, sought to wish their brother, pupil and buddy good luck.

"It was a neat situation," Zomer recalls, his normally friendly voice warming even more as he remembers that day. "He got a hit—that was so exciting! Well, just to see Derek on the field . . ." he pauses an instant. "About 10 minutes before the game started, we wanted to see Derek. We had to bribe the ushers to get down to the edge of the field. Just before the ballgame, Derek came out of the dugout to play catch with Don Mattingly. And that was just awesome to me! Don Mattingly! We're standing there alongside the field watching him get ready. Derek sees us, waves to us, turns to Mattingly and says 'Just a minute.' He comes over, greets us— gives his sister a big kiss—and with Mattingly waiting for him, says 'God, it's nice to have you here. Talk to you later. Now I have to go play ball.' Fantastic. Fantastic young man."

Now I have to go play ball. It sounds like he's walking off into the history and stirring it back to life.

However, it wasn't a golden season for Derek, not yet. He was a major-league Yankee for only a few weeks. Seen in hindsight, the events seem almost comical in their mixture of uncertainty and confusion but, at the time, he must have been wondering day to day where he would be playing, and for whom.

At that first home game, he played well, getting a single and a walk. There was a sure sign of confidence— he tried stealing bases. The Yankees won. Dorothy Connors, his grandmother whose love for the Yankees had set all this in motion, attended the game, surrounded by cheering Jeters. ("They had better seats than we used to get at the stadium,'' Jeter told a reporter. ''But I had the better view.'') Beneath all the congratulations was uncertainty.

The Yankees were waiting for Tony Fernandez to return any day now. They needed all their starting players off the disabled list—the team was running dead last in their division. It began to seem the Yankees were thinking of keeping Jeter on shortstop when Fernandez returned, and putting their veteran shortstop on second. This might explain why it took Fernandez longer to reappear than originally anticipated (''No comment,'' was his response when reporters confronted him with the move-to-second rumor). *Why* they wanted to keep Jeter around wasn't hard to explain: He was playing well, and the public and press were taking to him almost with open arms. Fans and reporters were calling Jeter ''The Kid,'' and already speculating about what a future this shortstop had with the Yankees.

If his major-league career wasn't yet confirmed, his star quality sure was. From the moment he arrived at Yankee stadium, the fan mail began coming in. Some of the letters were simply addressed, ''Derek Jeter, New York Yankees''—and they arrived with no problem. Even though he certainly hadn't yet demonstrated his strengths, the public recognized a player that was fascinating to watch. Right away, fans were waiting, pens at the ready. Other fans sent him baseball cards to sign, or requested autographs. More than a few of the letters (their pink-lined stationery, their curlicued script) suggested they were sent by girls and young women, but it is not known just when the first marriage proposal from a Jeter fan was opened by the no doubt amazed (even embarrassed) athlete. A longtime Jeter watcher recalls that early in his baseball life, when he was greeted by squeals from several admiring girls, Derek started and blushed deeply.

Being the new Yankee even helped Jeter with the cops. While Paul Morgan was covering chapter one in Jeter's Yankee life, reporter and shortstop were driving and accidentally pulled into the wrong toll station (they didn't have exact change). This is a ticketable offense and, sure enough, Officer Vinnie Zappulla approached, ready to write the driver up. Then, handed the license, he spotted the name. "Jeter," the officer said, then noticing the baseball cap. "I thought I recognized that name." He let Derek go without writing him a ticket.

Jeter's life, though full of new excitements, nonetheless resembled his old one. He was staying in a hotel in New Jersey with fellow Yankee rookie Mariano Rivera. He kept his usual hours: a late riser, seldom out of bed much before noon, everything he did was geared to being in the best condition for the next game. Despite the massive temptations of New York (and the hordes of women already eagerly noticing him) he seemed to have few of the problems associated with a sudden rise in success and attention. And the media covering him sometimes seemed as starstruck as the fans.

A week into his major league career, Jeter scored a milestone for a New York sports figure, and a sure indication he was not the usual rookie: He was the subject of a Mike Lupica column. Lupica, the doyen of New York sports columnists, is revered (at times feared) for his sharp, discriminating writing and clearly stated opinions. Obsessed with sports and with plenty of ideas of his own on how they should be run, Lupica is not exactly a kissing cousin of the Yankees. Over the years, he had been, by turns, inquisitive, critical, skeptical, even scornful of the moves of the Yankee organization and the conduct of its principal owner, George Steinbrenner. A Lupica column could be more stinging than any other, and readers digested them with a mixture of gasps, groans, and laughter. In a commercial for one of the newspapers he wrote for, Lupica was seen on a baseball diamond winding up for a hard pitch—but in his hands was not a baseball but a pad and pencil.

If he could dispatch an owner faster and more bloodily than Steinbrenner could one of his managers, Lupica was not as relentless to the athletes playing for the public. Toward players, he was certainly critical but, even when harsh, could demonstrate a fine eye and appreciation for the strength, diligence, and bravery of sportsmen.

He was also not above letting his own opinions on a team's personnel decisions be known, and agitating hard for those opinions. Where he stood on The Jeter Question was made clear in the title of his column, "Jeter Happy At The Stadium."

"Everything is happening fast for him these days, even the mail," Lupica began, standing by Jeter's locker room where the newest Yankee was already fielding not only questions from reporters and play advice from colleagues but the written attentions of admirers.

"If Fernandez is willing to move over to second base when he is ready to play, Jeter will stay around awhile," the columnist predicted. "If Fernandez doesn't want to play second, it is likely Jeter will go back to the minors."

Lupica was full of admiration for Derek's skills ("He is a big, exciting player at shortstop, even when he makes a mistake.") and he got supportive comments from catcher Mike Stanley and the great Mattingly, as well as from Pat Kelly, the second baseman whose injury had in part made Derek's debut possible. "There is a quiet grace about him, a sense that he belongs here," he continued, rhapsodizing and maybe rubbing it in. "Eventually, Jeter will go out to shortstop at Yankee Stadium and stay there a long time."

It was a fine column, and it didn't help. Six days after

filing it, Lupica and a crestfallen Yankee public watched as Derek Jeter was sent back to the minors, and Tony Fernandez returned to shortstop.

He had done well during his brief major league stint, earning a .234 batting average, making three doubles and six RBI in just 47 at-bats, and impressing management with his baserunning, as well as the agility and skill that people shook their heads over—just not the sort of performance you expect from a beginner. The Yankees, though, wanted the veteran Fernandez back at shortstop, and they didn't want Jeter sitting around waiting for another shot. (This, reportedly, is what Jeter was told by Buck Showalter.) So back to AAA he went, after a last game in which he hit a single and with a marvelous good-sport "Oh, well" on his departure making his new fans all the sorrier: "Tony [Fernandez] was the shortstop before he got hurt. I'm surprised they didn't send me out sooner."

A last comment made clear Jeter knew what he had done in these few weeks, and what he was certainly, someday, going to do: "It was good to get a taste of the big leagues. I'll be back eventually."

That is not the sad good-bye of a minor leaguer, but a major leaguer announcing himself. And, when he returned to AAA, his playing got anything but minor. (The Clippers found during his absence that spectators had been coming to see Jeter, and were disappointed when they learned he wasn't playing.)

Within two weeks, welcomed back and complimented, "Of all the guys I've worked with in minor league ball, he makes adjustments as well as anybody," hitting coach Gary Denbo told the *Columbus Dispatch*, he notched another accolade, making the AAA All-Star Game. In his league, he was rated tops in every category, ranking fifth in hitting and second in runs scored. But, even when he played this way, what he was really doing was waiting.

Meanwhile, back in New York, media and spectators were also waiting—with less patience. Bob Hertzel went on the warpath, filing a report on the Yankees' dismaying performance in Seattle in late August, and opening with "If Derek Jeter is the real goods—and there is nothing to make you think he is anything but—the time has come to promote him to the major leagues, stick him in the lineup, and see if he can help the Yankees win the American League wild-card berth that is rapidly slipping away.

"Anyone who has watched the Yankees sleepwalk through trips to Boston and the West Coast knows they need a kick in the rear. Jeter might be able to provide that kick with his youthful enthusiasm."

And Hertzel worded a convincing narrative of unease among the Yankees themselves—"We have reached the danger zone. It's got to turn and it's got to turn now," said Yankee captain Don Mattingly—accelerating the frustration by reporting a cool "I don't think that's a possibility at this time" from Buck Showalter when asked directly to bring Jeter back.

Lupica's column appeared just before Jeter was sent back to the minors. Hertzel's *Bergen Record* appeal was followed by happier news: after September 1, major league rules allow teams to expand their rosters with extra players. Derek Jeter was quickly brought back to the Yankees.

He actually didn't play very much. (Hertzel, obviously pleased with the turn of events but stymied by Jeter's inactivity, called Jeter "the invisible Yankee.") The Yankees were trying hard to score a wild-card slot in the division race. Showalter had been weathering the kind of rough season that usually hallmarks a determined effort to plug holes in a sagging team; maybe he just didn't feel it was right to test this obviously talented kid in such a tense environment. ''This is a tough time of year to be experimenting,'' he explained, sounding a little weary. Still, Showalter, a former minor-league short-stop himself, was encouraging to Jeter, urging him to use his time following his senior teammates closely.

Paul Morgan thinks he understands why they wanted Jeter around. ''He might have pinch run once, but [his return] was more like them saying to him, 'This is what it's like for you to be here, to be a Yankee player.' ''

''Everyone says you have to have patience,'' Derek said at the time. ''That's easier said than done, but it's out of my control. I can only control how I progress. My job is to be ready if I'm called on.'' Brief hopes were raised when Fernandez injured a knee, but Jeter remained on the bench. Anyway, Derek was a part of the Yankees' frazzled pennant race, if not playing in it. It would turn out to be a foretaste of what was coming. . . .

The New York Yankees' 1995 season ended with a defeat by the Seattle Mariners, but true mayhem in the Bronx was about to begin.

George Steinbrenner is known for several things. Two of them are getting what he wants and hating to lose. After a difficult season, the Yankees and their manager had pulled it together. For awhile, the Boss (as he is known) looked chipper. If things had improved some more, they might have won the season. They did earn the wild card, but were defeated in the playoffs by the Mariners. It was an impressive achievement in a rocky season, earning commendations for Showalter from press and public. But his team *didn't win*, and that's what counted more than anything else to Steinbrenner. Reporters waited breathlessly, all but hearing the axes being sharpened in the Yankees' front office.

Despite earning so much respect after a season of

intense effort, manager Buck Showalter was turned out, quickly. (In a typically graceless move, Showalter first learned of his "resignation" as Yankee manager when his wife heard the news on her car radio.) Negotiations with players old and new began, and they were not pretty. The public and their reporters responded to these goings on with shock and anger. Fortunately, none of this headrolling threatened Derek Jeter, but a Steinbrenner decision was to bring about one of the most crucial developments in the player's life.

On November 2, 1995, the Boss's new choice for manager of the Yankees was announced at a press conference in New York. It was Joe Torre, a distinguished player and the former manager of New York's other major league team, the Mets, whose often-hapless performances and thrilling World Series wins (1969 and 1986) only brought out more of New Yorkers' underdog love. Torre's career as a manager, however, had been (up to then) less than distinguished. The initial response, especially from the media, was first astonishment—Torre had just been booted from the floundering St. Louis Cardinals, and was considering a career not in the bullpen but as a broadcaster—then exasperation and even outrage. (The exacting Lupica, still smarting over Showalter's exit, practically went ballistic.) Tracking the strategic moves of a baseball team and the public response to those moves can resemble studying the progress of a world war.

What we need to know is that, back home in Kalamazoo, Jeter was still waiting, no doubt fairly confident, but he couldn't possibly have predicted the events that were about to happen, and the surprise and fulfillment that were awaiting him next season. And, out of the smoke and flames of the restaffed Yankees would come an opportunity for the young shortstop that would change his life.

He had been given some good advice, it turns out, from Buck Showalter: "Part of getting there is waiting for your opportunity," he told Jeter while the young man was cooling his heels in the Yankee dugout. And, in one of Bob Hertzel's boosters for Derek, lay an inadvertent assessment of what was about to happen in his life:

"If you are going to be a star player . . . there's no better place to start than in the most difficult of situations. That is what you will face your entire career."

Fifth Inning

Magic

"This whole season has been a dream come true!"

Anything Derek Jeter didn't yet know about the demands, risks, and rewards of baseball had to have been learned in his 1996 New York Yankees rookie season. It was full of superb performances and teamwork and sportsmanship. A diligent student of the game like Derek couldn't have asked for better lessons in how to play well, and win. The season also demonstrated a deeper truth, one frequently overlooked by young players because they haven't experienced it for themselves: It takes enormous reserves of strength, courage, confidence, intelligence, and heart to form the exact combination of power and daring and trust that makes up a team of real champions.

True, that season happened only three years ago, but it says something that, already, when baseball lovers compare favorite teams, players, years, when they get to the Yankees in 1996 . . . they pause and shake their heads in wonderment. It was that unforgettable.

Derek actually came close to missing the greatest season any rookie player could hope for. To explain what almost stopped him (and how chance and luck got him going again), we have to go back to 1995.

The moment of truth in Derek Jeter's career to date

occurred in late October, when George Steinbrenner, fuming over the near miss of his team at the end of the 1995 wild-card race, decided money, public opinion, and hurt feelings were not going to get in the way of his creating a season of champions *next* year. "It will take 10 years to rebuild this team from what George has done to it," critics complained. His choice for new manager, Joe Torre, was sneered at in print as "Clueless Joe," despite his being a native New Yorker and a veteran of nine All-Star games. But it was Torre's selection that clinched Jeter's chances.

If 1996 was a golden year for Derek, it was a crown of gold for Torre. The Marine Park, Brooklyn native had had a long career with plenty of ups and downs. Just before the Yankees made their move, he wondered if he would retire without ever making it to the postseason. He had had fine seasons as a player, earning the MVP award in 1971. As a manager, his record was bumpier. He had already managed the New York Mets for four years; in three of them, the team had finished the season dead last. He had also managed the Atlanta Braves, and been fired from *that* post by team owner and CNN mogul Ted Turner. The 1994 strike had aroused his sympathies and frustrations, and led to clashes with the owners of the St. Louis Cardinals, the team he was then managing. After being fired in 1995, in a way he and others found unnecessarily cruel, Torre considering returning to broadcasting. (A fine talker who can nonetheless be most terrifying when silent, Torre had tried sportscasting for the Angels in the 1980s and enjoyed it.) But when he was approached to manage the Yankees, he needed little encouragement to accept. He knew the organization was prepared to do anything for a championship, and that was just what Torre still wanted out of baseball.

There was already a World Series champion in the

Torre family—his older brother, Frank, had played for the Milwaukee Braves, and in 1957 the young Torre had watched his brother's team triumph against the Yankees in the Series. Thirty-nine years after that Yanks-Braves-Torre Series, at the end of the '96 season, the Yanks and the Braves would meet again, with the youngest Torre determined to win his own World Series ring. Getting a shot at the Fall Classic was the one missing piece Torre badly wanted to add to his career. The determination and sincerity evident in Torre's statements and actions sometimes seem an older, more seasoned version of Derek Jeter's.

If there had been any hesitation in Torre's mind about having to work with the Yankees' demanding owner, he gallantly omitted them for his memoirs, *Chasing the Dream*. He had already been interviewed for another Yankee position, and was about to put a thank-you note to Steinbrenner in the mail when senior Yankee advisor Arthur Richman sounded him out about the manager's job. A week later Steinbrenner himself called, to say "You're my man." It was a big step for Torre to take, especially since his wife was expecting a baby (their daughter was born in November 1995), and he certainly knew the job would not be easy. The owner later said he valued Torre's "mental toughness," a quality often native to New Yorkers, and one the midwesterner demonstrated plenty of himself. Steinbrenner was to learn Torre had another quality, one he might not have always valued: As a person close to the club puts it, "Steinbrenner can't get to Torre, and it can drive him crazy. But *nobody* gets to Torre." Behind the calm, watchful manner seen in the dugout clearly rests a resolve of steel. "Clueless Joe" set to work.

Torre meant it when he said he took the job because he knew the Yankee management wanted to be champions in 1996, and so did he. Part of a manager's job includes managing the reporters that circle teams like flies at a church picnic. They love the pickings, but they don't mind buzzing angrily about them, anyway. And, like all journalists, they are totally dependent on whom they cover—if their subjects don't behave in a newsworthy way, no copy gets filed. A former Yankee manager, Casey Stengel, put it perfectly when he noted, during a rough season, "Right now we pitchin' bad every place. Not hittin', not pitchin', and not fieldin' too good. And judging by what I read in the newspapers, the Yankee writers are in a slump, too."

Torre made it clear to Yankee reporters, at the outset of spring training in Tampa with his new team, that "I expect us to go to the World Series. I really like our chances." In their book on the '96 season, *Champions*, John Harper and Bob Klapisch, who were part of the local press corp following the new manager that several of them had scoffed at, described the effect of this remark: dead silence. They later understood the manager's daring: "Truth was, Torre didn't really need the job and was immune to the embarrassment and angst of being fired." He had been through all the humiliations and disappointments of the sport. Now, he was ready for its pinnacle, and had already determined how to get there: by forging a strong ensemble, a team of players who would work together as flawlessly and supportively as he, Torre, could manage. (Curiously, the team became a reflection of the manager's best qualities.) In recent seasons, baseball teams had become revolving doors of highly paid stars. Free agency had its virtues, but it also could have the disturbing effect of taking the emphasis off teamwork—as crucial an element to victory as the infallible swing of a top hitter or the laser-quick mitt of a shortstop. Torre wanted commited players for starters, and then they could work into becoming the greatest team of the season.

Putting such an ensemble of champs together wouldn't be easy, either. The loss of the team captain, Mattingly, who, when told his starting days were history, opted out, was a blow. But there were, fortunately, plenty of fine players approaching their prime on board—outfielder Paul O'Neill and pitcher David Cone in particular. New players were added, Tino Martinez (who had the daunting task of replacing Mattingly at first) and pitcher Andy Pettite, for example, both of whom would become close to Jeter and prove crucial to the fortunes of the Yankees. There was the splendid batter Bernie Williams who, with Torre's encouragement, got better and better over the season. And there would be a shortstop surprisingly equal to the rest of the team—once they finally picked him.

It wasn't that Yankee management didn't know enough about Jeter. General Manager Bob Watson had scouted him for the Astros when Derek was up for the draft in 1992, and at once spotted the potential. "You could tell even then that he was an intriguing talent," he recalled for *Yankees* magazine. "Just the instincts, the way he moved. There was something about him that didn't let you forget him."

Jeter had inspired confidence by his behavior after the disappointing 1995 finish, immediately returning to the Yankee complex in Tampa, to train. "I was at the complex every day," he told the *Kalamazoo Gazette*'s Paul Morgan. "I didn't go to Tampa to just hang out." Next season, for him, began as soon as the current season became last season. This must have been noticed in the Yankee offices.

Jeter was also fortunate enough to be part of a change in Yankee policy: Minor-league Yankees weren't often nurtured and eventually integrated into the New York team. As the 1996 season was in preparation, Steinbrenner and his managers engaged in frenzied searches for new players, spending millions in the process. They had also stopped automatically trading promising minor-leaguers, retaining and developing them instead. And the payoff in 1996 was astonishing: the season would not have been won without the achievement of their home-growns, which included Bernie Williams, Mariano Rivera, Andy Pettite. Not to mention their shortstop.

Actually, the Yankees had been having troubles in that position for a while. When he took the field on opening day 1996, Jeter would be the sixth shortstop to start for the Yankees in as many seasons. The team had not had an All-Star shortstop since Bucky Dent.

Initially, when surveying the options for the position, Torre was at a disadvantage in making an informed decision: He had never seen Jeter play. However, Yankee general manager Gene Michael had. A former shortstop, Michael had made up his mind on Jeter. Though still young and (comparatively) inexperienced, Michael argued that he was ready to play—ready to *start* as their shortstop.

"You're going to have to be patient with Jeter," Torre reports Michael warning him, during a conference call with Steinbrenner. "He's made some errors in the past, but he'll get better. He may not be ready from day one." Torre then heard Steinbrenner's comment: "I better not come up to Yankee Stadium until July. I might not like what I see."

In other words, this was a rough, and still not decisive, move on the Yankees' part. They were only giving the Kid a chance.

The decision might have been made easier knowing backup was close at hand, in case Derek proved not quite ready for the responsibility. Tony Fernandez would be on second, replacing Kelly (one of the athletes whose injuries in May 1995 had made Derek's temporary major-league promotion possible), who had had arthoscopic surgery the month before. If, God forbid, Derek choked or began to falter, they would not be entirely stranded.

The announcement, made on December 12, 1995, was not in the usual style, full of praise from the manager, confident quotes from the chosen player, and hosannas from strategically selected observers. At least a few news reports of the event set the right tone:

"The hype that has followed Jeter throughout a marvelous minor league career will finally be transferred to the Bronx on a full-time basis," wrote Jack Curry for the *New York Times*.

"Derek Jeter is going to be our shortstop going in," the new manager announced, but Curry noted he "did not sound overly thrilled about a rookie anchoring the infield." Torre waxed caution: "We want to take a look at it. The organization feels it's his time to play," arousing suspicion that this decision was not his own. In his memoirs, Torre is more upbeat.

"I liked him even before I saw him," he writes in *Chasing the Dream*. And he liked even more Derek's response to the news. The rookie knew exactly what his new situation was and how to handle it: "I'm going to get an *opportunity* to play shortstop."

As we've seen, Derek has never turned down, or made little of, opportunities. He seizes them as eagerly as he hones in on a ninth inning grounder burning grass toward him. So: Anyone like to guess how Derek's spring training performance would rate?

"We're going to try it," Torre went on to the *Times*. "We're not going to leave him out there without a safety net. We're going to be patient with him and see how it develops. But Tony Fernandez hopefully will be there in the event we need him to back up for us."

Note "hopefully" in that last statement. If genuine, it turned out to be optimistic. Spring training began in

Tampa on Monday, February 20, 1996. By the end of
day one, Tony Fernandez wanted out.

Seeing Jeter on the field must have been quite a sight,
for the veteran (who had actually been helpful to the
newcomer) went the next day to Yankee management to
request a trade, adding "I hope they do it soon."

Fernandez's position is one easy to sympathize with.
He was 33, had had several recent injuries, and now was
being replaced in the starting lineup by a 21-year-old.
He was in the final year of his Yankee contract. And,
he quickly realized, he was being used as a backup for
the newcomer and, as Bob Klapisch reported in the *Bergen Record*, "resent[ed] how quickly the Yankees have
reduced him to an insurance policy." Fernandez had
been told of Jeter's starting status by Torre in a December phone call; but now it was happening, and it must
have been galling.

To make things worse, the Yankees didn't want to
lose their insurance. Jeter was working hard, impressing
everyone with his effort, skills, and enthusiasm, but still,
anything could happen. Torre did damage control, urging patience on Fernandez's part, but it was quickly
looking like he would not be getting to his starting position as shortstop. Derek was doing very well.

When he finally got a good look at his long-shot
shortstop, Torre was impressed. He would be pleased,
he said, if Derek's defense got stronger and he attained
a batting average of .250. Back in Kalamazoo, a baseball
expert more experienced with this rookie raised eye-
brows at Torre's prediction.

"I was saying to myself, 'I know Derek is not going
to be satisfied with no .250,' " recalled his dad. Right
as always.

There was still a lot of work to do. What Derek knew
mattered as much as ability—consistency—was improved by the daily input of Torre and two coaches who

The rookie: Derek Sanderson Jeter, April 1996.
(© Jim Merithew/*Kalamazoo Gazette*, 1996)

Derek's parents, Charles and Dorothy Jeter, and sister Sharlee, encouraged and supported him every step of the way.

(© Jim Merithew/*Kalamazoo Gazette*, 1995)

Meeting an adoring, demanding public: signing autographs at Yankee Stadium. (© John Berger, 1998)

Media fascination with the Yankees' new short-stop was instantaneous. (© Jim Merithew/*Kalamazoo Gazette*, 1996)

"He already plays like a 10-year veteran": Baseball's young master at bat . . .

. . . whipping through one of his fabulous plays . . .

. . . and stealing yet another base.
(Three photos: ©
John Berger, 1998)

DJ vs. A-Rod: Playing opposite fellow shortstop and best baseball friend Alex Rodriguez of the Seattle Mariners. (© John Berger, 1998)

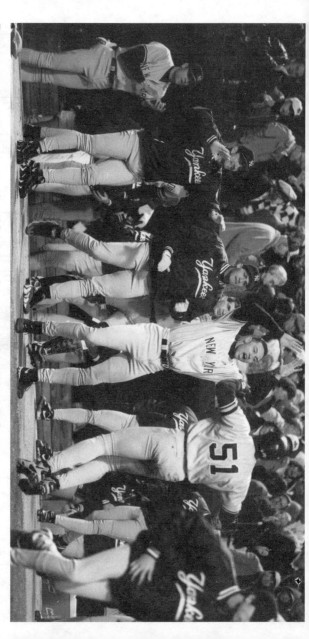

Dreams come true as the Yanks win the 1996 World Series. Derek congratulates Bernie Williams while teammates swarm the ballfield in celebration.

(© Globe Photos, Inc., 1998)

Celebrity head-on: former couple-of-the-moment Derek Jeter and Mariah Carey meet at Sean "Puffy" Combs' birthday party, November 1998.

"The game has been desperate for a matinee idol"
wrote one reporter . . . and now it has one.
(© John Berger, 1998)

had a big impact on Derek that year: Willie Randolph and Don Zimmer.

Randolph, a former Yankee (and once the team's captain), is shrewd and eloquent about the game and the strengths and shortcomings of its players, and he seems to have figured out his student right away. Zimmer, too, had spent a lifetime watching and playing: He had come out of retirement (having just started to get his Social Security checks!) at Torre's request, and throughout the season he would be seen beside Torre on the Yankees' bench, surveying the action and whispering suggestions into his manager's ear.

Coaches sometimes have to spend days, even whole portions of a season, correcting bad techniques and wrong reflexes in promising athletes to get them to their best playing level possible. This is not only true of rookies; as Derek was practicing and listening and learning, Dwight Gooden, a brilliant player with several years (and some hard knocks) under his belt, was dealing with pitching problems that would necessitate completely re-examining his windup pitch. When such work is successful, the results can be astonishing. Gooden emerged from the crisis to achieve a no-hitter, just when other circumstances threatened the Yankees' pitching staff. And Jeter—well, Jeter just kept getting better in practice and more exciting in play.

Derek's elevation to starting shortstop was like a replay of what happened in the minors. At the bottom rung, he fumbled, lost confidence, stumbled, and struggled. Then, he moved on to Greensboro, and quickly improved. Greater expectations and examples inspire him. The information he took in from watching more experienced players and being instructed by them was not too much for him to handle: It was just what he needed to come into his abilities. His new Yankee coaches, and the whole team, were going to be very glad to discover this aspect of him.

Randolph was delighted to find the hot young rookie a careful, willing, quick pupil. "Derek always listens, and when he hears something, he processes it and then uses it. I never hesitate to go to him and tell him something if I think he needs it. We have an understanding."

Even a prodigy like Jeter still has plenty to learn—as both the player himself and his coaches know well. "There are still times he seems like he gets caught by surprise in the field," Randolph continued, to the *Daily News*. "He could be more selective when he's hitting. But all that's just experience."

Randolph was already aware that Jeter was a Yankee. He made the following observation later in the summer, but it wouldn't be surprising if he noticed it during spring training. "You can tell by the way a guy carries himself—like he belongs."

Others certainly were. Early reports were worried for the rookie: The Yankees were aiming high; could this kid really keep up with them? Was it fair to ask any beginner, however talented, to meet such a challenge in his first season, when he's probably just getting used to being a major leaguer?

Jeter, like every other team member, knew what the prize was. Torre had gathered his players together and, as he wrote in his memoirs, spelled it out for them.

"Men," he said, "every single one of my coaches has been to the World Series. I haven't. I plan to rectify that this year. I'm determined as hell to get there." He laid out his own code of ethics: to communicate directly with each player and not manage through the media; to eliminate the extra tensions and worries that a team of competitive players always feels; and to keep focus on the goal—winning the Series. "The only thing I'm interested in is the way we perform on the field, and I'm going to make it as tension-free as possible so that we can devote all of our energy to that.''

It was a heady atmosphere of ambition and deadly earnestness, the toughest kind in any team. It was at just this moment that the Yankees, already pleased by the performance of their young shortstop, almost drew back and removed him.

Earlier in February, a Jeter enthusiast had shown a videotape of the player in action to both Steinbrenner and Torre. Both, he reported, were pleased by what they saw. But there was still uncertainty, at least in the owner's mind, about plunging Derek into so momentous a season.

When Steinbrenner doubted, it was wise to worry. A revolving door of fired personnel could testify to the power of his anger or dissatisfaction. Although not the exclusive owner of the team (he had bought them, for $10 million, as part of a dozen general partners in 1973), he was the man who made the decisions. And he seemed to have had trouble committing to Jeter as his starting shortstop.

A week or so before the season opener, the owner suddenly walked into Torre's office and voiced doubts—''My advisers tell me they don't think Jeter is ready to play,'' according to Torre. Another source has Steinbrenner asking Torre in the same meeting if they should not play it safe and arrange a trade for a veteran shortstop, one with a proven performance record in the majors. The sense one gets is that Steinbrenner wasn't so much doubting Jeter as wondering if he was simply asking too much even of this talented beginner. The manager himself was still not entirely sure about the readiness of their shortstop, but Derek had already worked so hard, Torre was confident enough to answer Steinbrenner with ''Well, it's too late for that now, folks.'' ''We had already made our commitment,'' he wrote of the encounter. Later, to a reporter, he said "Sooner or later a player can no longer benefit from being in the minor leagues. It's Derek's time."

Did Derek know about this close shave? We don't know. He is so perceptive he probably didn't have to be told; he perhaps sensed their concerns. If so, he responded to them in the best possible way: impressing his colleagues the moment the season began.

The relationship with Torre was crucial to Derek's success. In terms of their passion for work and dedication to the game, the rookie shortstop and the new Yankee manager seem versions of the same player at different ages. Mario Cuomo, former governor of New York and former minor-league centerfielder, is a keen observer of baseball. He noticed this sharing of values and achievement between Torre and Jeter quickly. "Torre and Jeter share those virtues—so it's easier for a Jeter to play for a Torre. I played against Torre's brother [Frank], and I recognize the quality."

Now Derek was a Yankee, and he had his own number, 2. As a student, this enormously gifted, lucky kid played with a 13 on his back. (One hopes that the Jeters found this funny.) He was number 24 in Greensboro. When he became a New York Yankee, both those numbers were taken, so he was given number 2. Paul Morgan points out, "It was the only single-digit player number the Yankees didn't yet have in the Hall of Fame. I wonder if they realized that when they gave it to Derek." The number 2 had been worn by another legendary shortstop (and coach), Frank Crosetti. In the batting order, he was placed ninth, again to keep him from feeling pressured, and because his manager wanted his energies locked on defense.

The Yankees' season commenced on April Fool's Day, in Cleveland. Opening Day should have intimidated Derek but, in fact, Torre was approached by his shortstop, who, rather than begging assurance from his boss, asked "You okay?" remembering he himself was not the only Yankee beginner that day. This ability to make the right gesture was something about Jeter that Torre clearly recognized immediately, and adored. Another was Derek's always referring to his manager as "Mr. Torre," a practice that, three seasons and two World Series later, Derek continues (although Torre adds that Jeter's respectful "Mrs. Torre" to his wife makes her feel old).

On Opening Day, he got his first major-league home run off Cleveland Indian Dennis Martinez, startling everyone in the stadium, including veteran Yankee player and announcer Phil Rizzuto. Derek earned his first Rizzuto "Holy cow!" as his hit zipped out of the park and he sped the bases. The Yankees won that game 7-1.

Torre began to wonder if worrying about his shortstop making .250 was really necessary. He said in retrospect that he was so concerned about the pressures of a big season on a kid just out of the minors that in spring training he concentrated on defense with Derek. Then the Kid started hitting and fielding like a seasoned adult:

"I received two pleasant surprises on Opening Day: a huge good-luck basket of goodies from my friend Big Julie Isaacson and a stunning performance by Jeter.... [O]nce the season started, it was as if he jumped into a phone booth and changed into a Superman costume. The rookie made a great catch of a pop fly and hit a home run—signs of things to come."

"I was lucky," Jeter said, with the typical modesty no one, least of all the media, seems to tire of. "The important thing was that we won the game. It's good to get off to a good start, but we have 161 more games and you have to build on this start."

In this incredibly competitive atmosphere, with the entire team aware that the club's reputation was on the line and could be redeemed only by a postseason run, their youngster was performing with the skill and discipline of a veteran. "He plays like he's been in the game ten years," was a frequent comment. People couldn't understand it. They knew Jeter was gifted, they'd known he was eventually coming to play but, now that he was in front of them, they were shocked. In a team less bent on absolute victory, Derek would probably have been made much of right away, but there was a season to be won and a series to be fought for, so everyone's mind was kept on playing better and winning more. This probably turned to his advantage, for Derek is always at his best when focused on his work. More specifically, improving his work.

In his memoirs, Torre writes of Jeter with real admiration, calling him his "unflappable kid." "He plays every game, including the World Series, like it's Saturday morning on the sandlots of Marine Park. . . . Keeping up his work habits will be key."

But it wasn't just in the Yankee dugout that this delighted recognition was registering. ESPN's Dave Campbell assessed the rookie player shrewdly: "Jeter brings a lot of intangibles to the Yankees. The first six batters in their lineup are guys who take a lot of pitches and work the count and that's one of the hidden keys to the Yankees' lineup and Jeter was first in pitches seen in the American League.

"He really knows how to work the pitcher and work the count and that's become a trademark of the Yankees and a big reason why they're able to get rid of starters by the fifth inning so many times. That's 'professional' hitting."

On April 9, despite freezing weather and even snow, Yankee Stadium opened for business. They won again, and Derek homered, hearing for the first time that ecstatic Yankee Stadium roar celebrating his score. Soon the roar would begin as soon as he stepped up to home plate to bat. The shortstop, and his team, were off and running.

Well, you probably know what happened that year. Maybe you were watching at home, or in the stadium, sharing the mounting excitement as the New York Yankees steamed through the first half of the season with an ever-higher record of wins (they were 26-11 by the beginning of May), then suddenly flagging a bit. Maybe you wondered just what happened when manager Torre called his famous ''red-ass meeting'' at the end of May and made his anger at his team's dwindling performance very plain. Maybe the roller coaster of the rest of the season kept you as breathless as it did others, when the Yankees' lead shrank to two-and-a-half games, and Steinbrenner began looking like he had spent a fortune on a pile of lemons. And maybe you almost couldn't stand the stress of the Yankees persevering, coming from behind in game after game, physically uniting into this powerful, almost fierce, playing machine, and winning again until they entered the playoffs in triumph. Maybe, when it was all over, you were one of the nearly four million worshippers cheering the team as they paraded down the Canyon of Heroes.

It was a season that was thrilling, hair-raising, exhausting, and ultimately awesome to watch—and, no doubt, to play. New York became a baseball town again in a way it had not been for almost a generation. Baseball mattered to the entire city, attracting the attention and anxiety of even nonfans. As sometimes happens, common interest or hope drew its inhabitants into the singleminded enthusiasm of a small town.

This isn't a chronicle of that season (though some

moments in it will prove too delicious to resist). What we want to know is, what did Derek do that season, what did he learn, and how did he feel about it?

The first question is the easiest. He performed way, way above Yankee expectations, closing the season with a .314 batting average, 582 at-bats, 183 hits, 104 runs, 78 runs batted in, and 10 home runs. He had a 17-game hitting streak, the longest by a Yankee rookie since Joe DiMaggio, 60 years previously. He contributed totally, irreplaceably, and unexpectedly (still a beginner) to his team's success. And he became, in one season, one of the most talked-about and popular athletes—no, people— in New York.

It wasn't an uninterrupted series of triumphs, though. He was a great young player, but not (Torre's speculation to the contrary) Superman. He had his problems. There was still some doubt circling Derek, first in the clubhouse, but also in the stands and the press. "Terrific kid, but can he last all summer?"

On March 19, Derek might have been asking that of himself. *Bergen Record* reporter Bob Klapisch witnessed a poignant moment: The young shortstop had come to grief the day before in a game opposite the White Sox, striking out three times. On this day, Jeter sat in the visitor's clubhouse, watching the reporter as he left an interview with Torre in his office, and wondering, ruefully, just what had transpired. "What's he saying?" Jeter asked Klapisch of Torre, perhaps envisioning a demotion to the minors.

"I mean, I was right there, right on it," Klapisch records Jeter saying. "What can I say?" He tries to explain: "I've never had a good spring training hitting. If I was ever really judged on the way I hit in Florida, I'd still be in A-ball."

What's even sweeter about this story is that the reporter had just heard reassuring words from Torre: They know Derek will have moments like this. They also know he has marvelous soft hands as shortstop, and unexpected power at bat, and they are prepared to hang on and bring him along as well as they can. The image of the new Yankee so disappointed, insisting (maybe primarily to himself) that "I'll be fine. I will. I really will," is a moving one.

Jeter would not be the only Yankee suffering setbacks that season. Another reason this rookie year couldn't have been better for Derek, as a player and a person, was the scope of its human drama. Despite the triumphs on the field, events in the lives of players and even their relatives put those victories in perspective and, at times, made them hard won.

Early in the season the team's best pitcher, David Cone, was aware of a numbness in his pitching hand and a sense that something was not quite right with his arm. After a lot of speculation and worry, he submitted to an angiogram, a long, painful test to determine what was wrong. At first, it was thought that some lifestyle changes (exercise, technique) might address the problem. By early May, despite some fine pitching, the numbness persisted and another angiogram was scheduled. The team was winning against the Detroit Tigers when the Yankee physician and Torre heard the diagnosis. The game won, they gathered the team together for the news, which wasn't good: Cone had an aneurysm in his right (pitcher's) arm. An aneurysm (an abnormal filling of blood in the wall of a vein) if undetected and untreated, is fatal. Cone was immediately undergoing surgery, in which the aneurysm would be removed and a bit of blood wall from one of his legs would be used as a replacement. He was, needless to say, out of the game, probably for a while, very possibly for the whole season, and, possibly, forever.

Torre recalled the clubhouse became filled with

glassy eyes as the doctor patiently explained Cone's situation to his stunned teammates. "No one believed for a second that the Yankees could survive an extended loss of Cone," Bob Klapisch and John Harper wrote, "and now it seemed unlikely he would be back at all in '96." The club regrouped, but it was rough. Cone endured a three-hour surgery and began the slow recovery, but no one knew how long that would take, or if he would ever be the great pitcher he was again.

As the newest guy on the team, Jeter couldn't have been unaffected by this. Baseball had always been a wonderful game for him, a place where he could make things work out. But he wasn't dumb: He knew life hit plenty of curves even to those who tried to live it well and conscientiously; hard knocks are dealt especially to the ambitious, a trait Cone shared with him. "I had pitching taken away from me for the first time," Cone said later of his ordeal. Losing the game for good was something probably beyond Jeter's imagination—and, one hopes, a loss he will have to face only after a long, satisfying career. Cone's rallying, his slow recovery and determined exercising, his insisting he would play *this* season, rejoining the champions, became a lesson in courage. His return on Labor Day, pitching seven no-hit innings, was one of the most triumphal moments of a season packed with them.

The man the Yankees relied on to help them through the loss of Cone provided another lesson in bouncing back, and enduring. Dwight Gooden had had as much promise in his beginnings as Jeter, but he hadn't his strong background, and wasn't able to handle the tension and exposure of the sport as well as Jeter did (and would). Erratic behavior and drug abuse had almost destroyed him. Now he was trying to come back, and was having trouble finding his command of pitches. The timing couldn't have been worse—the Yankees had wanted him to rebound, but now with Cone in recovery they *needed* Doc Gooden.

The pitcher struggled to improve his arm. It was an observation from coach and former Yankee Mel Stottlemyre that proved key: He urged Gooden to simplify his windup, streamlining his arm and leg, putting everything into straightforward delivery. It worked. He began starting for the Yankees again, and doing well. Then, during a game against the Seattle Mariners, Gooden pitched a no-hitter that became one of *the* stories of an already storied season. Jeter was one of the ecstatic Yankees who swarmed around the pitcher, carrying him off the field in triumph.

The whole season was like that—filled with lessons in how to be better, how to get up when hit hard, and how to prevail. If baseball had often seemed like life to Derek Jeter, he was witnessing a lifetime's worth of travails in the efforts of his teammates, and a lifetime's worth of instruction from their excellent play.

By August, however, their 10-game lead was shrinking. Torre applied more spurs to the team's efforts, but they still didn't seem as strong. Steinbrenner started looking doomed again.

Jeter, however, was flourishing. He kept surprising the Yankees and their fans, and then doing better and surprising them some more. His eagerness to play had complete expression on the ballfield, and his play had little flourishes that watchers found delightful. He would leap in the air with a dancer's grace to catch a ball. He would spring up and catch and throw to first to make a double play, all in one fast and seamless move, and a watcher's immediate response would not only be ''Wow! He did that!'' but ''God, how beautiful!'' People didn't just applaud or yell when he did one of these things—they gasped at how marvelously this young man could play. And, if you looked quickly, you could see the same openmouthed astonishment on faces peering from the Yankee bullpen, or looming from the manager's box.

Yet he didn't seem to be taking the sudden flush of adulation to heart at all. Maybe coping with this attention required more late-night phone calls back to Kalamazoo, but he earned his teammates' respect by handling it all so well. He was in a tricky position— some could have begrudged him the success and attention. He was so unchanged by it, though, that no resentments seemed to fester. Instead, he was appreciated, and teased, and respected.

This respect was shared by Torre. At times, the manager watched warily as his new star shortstop would happily come out of the bullpen before the game to sign everything in sight held out by grateful fans—especially female fans. The horde of bright smiles meeting Jeter at these moments must have been so blinding, it's a wonder he didn't resort to sunglasses. Torre later admitted to finding even more disturbing another practice of his rookie's: answering comments and questions made by admirers as he swung on deck, ready to take his turn at bat. Even sports observers found this surprising; watching Derek smile, respond, sometimes even go over to talk (especially to children; his ability to form an instant bond with any child is infallible), they would think he was going too far. But Derek seemed to have the ability to switch his concentration on and off instantly; when it was his turn to bat, he stepped to the plate completely focused, ready. Torre didn't intervene, although he hinted if he thought this practice became distracting he would.

Derek at bat is hardly a classic figure. He scrunches his 6'3" self into a deep crouch, his butt sticking far out. His legs appear to vibrate, his feet almost hum, as if impatient to be running to first base. His elbows seem rubbery. He grips the bat firmly yet, above his head, the bat end wiggles constantly, as if he's trying to stir the air above his head with it. His face brightens; all of it seems to open wide. The eyes get very, very clear; even his nose seems to sharpen. The mouth takes on the set of a determined boy's. The pitch comes, and Jeter instantly calibrates what it is and how to respond. When it's a ball, he waits, and his feet shift some more in impatience. He doesn't like to let a ball go without a swing at it. (This overeagerness is one of his few consistent faults.) He stares bluntly but not meanly at the pitcher; glares and eye games are standard between pitcher and prey, but Derek doesn't seem to go in for that drama. Another pitch, a strike. He never likes one, but doesn't argue with the umpire, keeping his comments (if any) brief and stating them mildly, like pointing out a red light to someone about to cross the street. Another pitch, and it's a hit, and he instantly comes to life. A split-second look up and he's off, the legs now at full, long length, the arms not so much pumping the air as flying along on it. A single, and he bounces back to first, looking like a kid as he immediately gets into stealing mode. ("That is one of the happiest men I've ever seen," a fan said once, watching Jeter on TV look innocent before stealing second.) A double, and he keeps charging, a single look for the ball propelling him forward. And when he gets home (on his own run or someone else's) he rounds third and returns with a look of gentle but definite pride.

Funny as he looked, he was batting great. Torre moved him to the top of the batting order, and his average, as if in gratitude, soared to .449. "I'll hit wherever they want me to, as long as it's not tenth," Derek said cheerfully.

Everything about the guy on the field is immensely reassuring, because whatever he does seems motivated by joy. It's an illustration of what his father sensed very early: Baseball is his world, and he looks completely at home in it.

This can make getting mad at him difficult. A Jeter error is seldom met with a round of boos from the home crowd; more often, it elicits sighs of disappointment and understanding murmurs. ("Poor Derek, he works *so* hard. It must be tough to have missed that one.") This natural expression of sympathy can extend even to Derek's manager.

During their midsummer slump, the Yanks lost a game in Chicago—Jeter, in the eighth inning of a tie with powerhouse Cecil Fielder at bat, tried to steal one base too many. He got caught, and thrown out. In the dugout, Torre was pissed, not only at his overeager runner, but at himself. "I should have given him the sign *not* to run," he tells us in his book. "I made the mistake of assuming that a rookie would know to let Cecil swing the bat in that situation." The momentary villain trotted back to the dugout. Torre doesn't go over to Derek; he's still so mad at the out he has to say to himself "He's still a kid; calm down," though he wants to go over and scream at him. Were the other players and coaches watching this, and were they expecting the shortstop to make himself scarce? If so, they must have been startled when Derek looked in Torre's direction, saw that boiling mad face, and responded by coming over and sitting right next to him. The manager duly yells at his shortstop, probably at this point because it's his job to (how could you not yell at someone who comes over and *allows* you to like that?) more than from the rage he had been feeling. Torre concludes his description of this incident with the final admiring comment, "Jeter constantly impressed me with his poise."

By the time the Yankees clinched the Eastern Division title against Milwaukee on September 25, the score of the game was an incredible 19-2 and the Yankees were looking like champions again. Then they went up against the Texas Rangers in the American League Division Series, and got trounced in their first game, 6-2. Jeter didn't handle his at-bats well that night, getting out with bases loaded and two outs in the sixth. Typically, the next night, he played much better, scoring the winning run at the end of a 12-inning marathon that the Yanks took 5-4. This was when he most showed his rookieness: the sudden deflation of achievement followed by a swift, eye-blinking rebound. "Consistency" was still not that consistent. Torre told writer Steve Adamek, "You start talking to guys, it looks like you're calling attention to a specific problem. Jeter's different than most young kids. I don't think he's going through anything where he can't function at the plate."

Two games later, the Yanks were through with the Rangers, and the American League Championship Series awaited—against their sworn enemies, the Baltimore Orioles. Derek Jeter made a home run in Game 1 that will be remembered as one of the most unusual in baseball history.

It wasn't so much how well he hit it, but who caught it. In the eighth inning, before a packed Yankee Stadium, Jeter swung and hit a pitch from the Orioles' Armando Benitez. The ball sailed out and almost over the right-field wall. The crowd's roar lowered as they feared outfielder Tony Tarasco would catch it. Down it went, and suddenly Tarasco looked astonished. "It was like magic," he said later. "I was about to catch the ball, and it disappeared."

But the ball *had* been caught—by a twelve-year-old kid playing hooky. Jeffrey Maier from Tappan Zee, New Jersey, with flawless timing, reached out from the stands and got it. Below him, a furious Tarasco pointed upwards, yelling about what he saw as interference. Umpire Richie Garcia made the home-run signal, at which point the sound in the stadium became deafening. Jeter's hit had been a beauty, and the kid in the stands catching the ball (and the umpire not ruling interference) didn't seem to the crowd like a bad call—it was a sign from God.

There *was* something strangely magical about that moment. The adult Jeter hit the ball, it almost sailed out of the park, and it got caught by a boy like Jeter once was, a boy who loved baseball and whose ready hand and glove changed the history of the Series. If you look quickly at the video of that moment, you can almost imagine the boy Jeter catching the ball sent right to him by Jeter the man.

Meanwhile, back on earth, Orioles were swooping on the offending umpire with furious cries. Their manager, Davey Johnson, got so worked up (the utter delight of 57,000 onlookers couldn't have helped) that the umpire he was bellowing at threw him out of the game. Tony Tarasco, denied the thrill of catching the ball, had to be held down by teammates. Above the fracas, Jeffrey Maier was being hailed as a hero.

"An angel in the outfield," people said. Derek said just the right things when pressed on this subject. "That [catch] didn't win the game. Bernie did." (It is true Jeter scored the tying run, and Bernie Williams, later, the winning one.) He did allow one glint through. "Do I feel bad?" he asked the *Bergen Record*. "We won the game. You should ask them that." Them being, needless to say, the Orioles.

The game over, the uproar only increased. The Orioles watched the replay of the catch again and again, while their owner prepared to file a complaint and their fans muttered in indignation. New York's mayor, Rudolph Giuliani, whose obsession for law and order rivals his Yankee fixation, didn't exactly have little Jeffrey reprimanded. Maier was treated like a little Buddha when he appeared before a gleeful host and public on *The David Letterman Show*. Joe Torre, sounding reasonable, commented "Controversial calls are part of the game," but then admitted that as long as *this* call was official, he would accept it.

Professional scolds like conservative George Will loudly deplored the immorality of the catch—the kid was skipping school, interfered with the game, and so on—and soon poor Jeffrey Maier and his parents must have wondered if, for intercepting a baseball, he'd wind up in jail. The collective delight of New Yorkers, and the refusal of an appeal on the umpire's ruling, eventually settled the matter.

That miraculous moment cast a pall over the Orioles for the entire Series. They got short-term revenge in Game 2, but were then dispatched in three more outings. After Derek clinched the final out of the winning ALCS game against the Orioles, his parents, who had come to see the win, celebrated and then made the long drive home to Kalamazoo from Baltimore. "We had a chance to reflect," Dr. Jeter recalled to Rafael Hermoso. "It was like seeing him in Little League. You might not see it, but his enthusiasm, his joy, I can look back and see the same mannerisms from Little League."

When the Yankees took a seven-day rest and then turned their attention to the Atlanta Braves and the World Series, they were jubilant. Joe Torre had met the moment of victory over the Orioles with tears. It wasn't only the thrill of winning—of all the roller coasters endured by the Yankees in a mountainous season, his was the wildest.

All along, family problems had been tugging at the manager's attention. His brother, Frank (the World Series champion), was ill, and eventually diagnosed with heart trouble. It took Torre every bit of persuasion to get his exhausted, despairing brother to New York and a heart specialist. Frank would spend eleven weeks in the hospital, awaiting a heart for transplant. Before this happened, Torre's *other* brother, Rocco, after watching a Yankee game at home, collapsed—a heart attack—and died. Torre's family has been his foundation (even more than baseball), and the death was heartrending. He put his score card from that final game his brother watched into his coffin, along with a Yankee cap. But Torre kept going. His tears the night of the ALCS moved many to fill his answering machine with heartfelt congratulations.

Now, he was finally at the threshold of the challenge he had dreamed of since watching Frank Torre play in the 1957 World Series. It had taken 39 years, he had played, managed, won awards, and been fired—but he was here. If the Yanks won, Torre would be the first native New Yorker to manage them victoriously in a World Series. The whole city was proud and anxious at once.

Jeter seemed ready even for this challenge. And before Game 1, there was a moment to remind him how far he had come.

As a boy he had waited in a parking lot to get an autograph from a Yankee idol, Dave Winfield. Jeter has cited the star's autobiography, *Winfield: A Player's Life,* as his favorite book. It seems almost a guide to the kind of hardworking career his young fan dreamed of having and then made real:

"I know it sounds corny [Winfield wrote] but I feel that more than any one thing, it's my attitude that has made my life work, that's enabled me to achieve the success I've had. It's also something I look for in other people, the ballplayers I play with, the people I spend time with outside the game." It sounds like Derek surrounded by '96 Yankees.

Winfield's effect on Jeter extended not only to his conduct, but his founding his own not-for-profit foundation in partial emulation of Winfield's example. Now, entering Yankee Stadium to play his first Fall Classic, he was approached by yet another fan: Dave Winfield. Now, his idol wanted to express his own admiration for Jeter's game. The moment must have been dizzying with emotion, even more poignant than when Jeter sees countless young people reaching for his own hand to shake, admiring him as much as he admired Winfield and other athletes who motivated his own excellence.

Jeter had gotten through a testing rookie season with no major lapses in playing or appearance. However, there are limits to even the most adroit tightrope walkers, and even he must have reeled after Game 1 of the Series, when the Atlanta Braves demolished the Yanks, 12-1. As Wade Boggs put it, "We ran into a buzzsaw."

Torre tells us that before Game 2, he addressed his troops and told them, "We've played and beaten better offensive teams than Atlanta. . . . There's no reason why we can't beat this team." A little before that, into Torre's office hurried George Steinbrenner, who (for once) could not be blamed by anyone for being agitated. "This is a must game," he said, and when his manager answered, "You should be prepared for us to lose again tonight," the owner was speechless. Torre explained that he felt things would pick up for the team when they got to Atlanta. He was hopeful that they would sweep the three games there, and then return to Yankee Stadium to clinch the Series.

Game 2's score was not so mortifying, but it was still a defeat. The Braves creamed them again, 4-0. And Derek got injured. Struck on the left wrist by a fastball from pitcher Greg Maddux, he was immediately looked at by Torre, but Jeter stayed in. The sore wrist plagued him, leading Derek to botch a catch in the sixth inning. There was a worry that he was really hurt and would be pulled from Game 3; the Yankee doctor checked him out carefully. Jeter did go on, and played well. Torre credited him, throughout the season, postseason, and Series, for being the player who started rallies that saved the Yankees in game after game. The team had an amazing ability to weather misfortune in early innings and then come back, strongly, sometimes staggeringly, in the later innings— a quality they would perfect in the 1998 Series.

Also amazing was Torre's ability to project the Series outcome. His three-wins-in-Atlanta, one-in-New-York forecast was exactly what happened. It was as if the team needed those two losses to gather their forces to become, again, the unbeatable Yankees, the team that had triumphed for generations and was now starting a new wave of achievement.

Before the finale, there was one more bend in the road. The day before Game 6, Frank Torre finally got his new heart. The long surgery seemed to be successful, and his cardiologist suggested Frank might even be well enough to watch the game on the intensive-care-unit television set. Jokes immediately started as to how Game 6 would be a great test for Frank's new heart.

It wasn't only Frank's heart that got a workout. The Yankees, their manager, and their shortstop were nine innings away from being World Champions.

This was it, this was the last perfect episode in the scenario of his lifelong dream, but Derek didn't seem paralyzed by fear and responsibility. "Derek doesn't see the postseason as something different," remarked manager Torre, who certainly did. Jeter arrived that day and listened to music through headphones (Mariah Carey, according to *Sports Illustrated*), as he put on his uniform and cleats. Far from dreading the moment of baseball history that could define his career for good or ill, he joked and looked as eager to take the field as ever. "I do have butterflies, especially while I'm waiting for a game to start," he once claimed, perhaps baffled at the constant citing of his steely nerves by interviewers and colleagues.

"The thing that sets Derek apart is that he's not afraid to fail," third baseman Charlie Hayes, who caught the final out of the Series in Game 6, said at the start of it. "He wants the ball hit to him in the last inning of the last game, with the whole World Series at stake." Even in such a potentially lethal situation as Game 6, baseball was still, most of all, *fun*.

If Derek found it fun that night, for everyone else it was nerve-racking.

The Yanks rallied splendidly in the third, scoring three runs to increasing fan delirium. Then, the Braves fought back, scoring their own run. Torre played for one more time his 6-2-1 pitching combination: taking the original pitcher out after six innings, substituting Mariano Rivera, whose calm and sure arm were almost too cruel to inflict on enemy batters so late in the game, and then pulling *him* and sending in John Wetteland in the ninth. The final inning didn't kill Frank Torre, and that's a wonder: Ahead by two, the team watched wide-eyed as Wetteland handed out a strikeout, followed by two singles, and then another strikeout. A single by Brave Marquis Grissom brought in another run. One out, one run separated the Yankees from victory or loss. When the next Brave, Mark Lemke, hit a pop foul behind third base, the crowds, the players, and millions more watching on television seemed to hold an enormous collective breath.

Then, Charlie Hayes caught the ball, and the breath

turned into an explosion of delight. Derek joined the pileup of Yankees on the field. Momentarily immobile in the dugout, Torre and Don Zimmer seemed thunderstruck. A moment before the reality of victory, Zimmer had whispered, "This one's for Frank," to his manager. Then, as they came to themselves and ran out to the pileup in the field, a suggestion Zimmer had made earlier struck Torre as the right thing to do; so he gathered his players together and led them in a victory lap around the perimeter of the stadium as a gesture of thanks to the fans. Together one more time, the group that had given the world a definition of the value of teamwork jogged around the ballfield built by and for the hard labor and inspiration of almost 75 years of Yankees. (The run completed, Zimmer gasped to Torre that he had meant the victory lap to be a *walk*!)

In the clubhouse, amid flashing cameras and video lights, speeches, a brief appearance from the Boss, and sprayed bottles of champagne, running excitedly back and forth, was Derek Jeter. For the first time all season— at the end of the journey—he seemed disoriented, even in a daze. He just kept dashing around, occasionally stopping to sip champagne. "I'm just so happy," he finally said, his experience struggling into words. "I'm just so happy. It's just magic. Just magic."

That wasn't fully true; one hopes that at this moment of triumph he knew it was not just magic at all, but the fruition of his own faith and effort. This was the moment of fulfillment his entire life had been dedicated to. Everything had come together for him with a perfection we demand from movies or novels but hardly dare hope for in real life. The shortstop position; the wondrous season, made more so by his own abilities; the small boy grown up meeting his idol, and discovering that idol had become his admirer; the champagne dash of victory in the clubhouse. He had dared to hope, and it had happened. His dream born sixteen years ago—in the stadium he had triumphed in, and which he and others now called his home— had been brought into the world.

Soon he would be honored, with the rest of the Yankees, by a ticker-tape parade down the Canyon of Heroes (New York's financial district), the same route which had honored previous Yankees (and the Mets), and war heroes, and idols of the century like swimmer Gertrude Ederle, flyer Charles Lindbergh, and astronaut John Glenn (twice). As many as four million grateful New Yorkers would turn out on October 29, 1996, to thank Derek and his colleagues. Led by a beaming Mayor Giuliani, New York would award each Yankee with a key to the city. And Derek would be named Rookie of the Year. And Most Valuable Player (MVP) of the Series. And fly home to his parents' triumph and his entire community's salute in Kalamazoo . . . a series of blessings, icing on the cake of his wonderful year—still his first year in major-league baseball . . .

What was left for someone, 22 years old, still a youngster practically, who had already fulfilled his dream? In the raptures of postseason 1996 some Jeter fans, still wildly infatuated with their new idol, sounded a bit worried: Was the beginning of his achievement so complete it would prove the end? Would getting what he wanted his whole life so quickly and perfectly prove not a blessing, but a curse?

People who knew Derek well probably were not as worried. Victory is one thing, perfection another. Any doubts as to his ability to imagine more for himself after this season's fulfillment, to rise to the next challenge next season were answered when Derek won Rookie of the Year.

"This whole season has been a dream come true," he stated; but then added "I'm still dreaming. . . . I hope we can do it a few more years."

Sixth Inning

Jetermania!

Q: What was the toughest thing that you had to handle in New York?

A: Probably the media. You're under a microscope all of the time, so you've got to try to keep a level head. (ESPNEWS, Nov. 1, 1996)

One night, while driving home after a Yankees game, Derek Jeter began darting in and out of traffic like a racing demon. No, he wasn't having fun on the FDR Drive, or entertaining or thrilling a passenger—he was trying to lose autograph hounds who had tailed him all the way from the Bronx.

"It can definitely be a scary situation," he later told Pedro Gomez of *The Arizona Republic*. "The FDR is not an easy road to maneuver in and out of. But I have no way of knowing what those people's intentions are. You have to be careful, and that not only goes for New York but anywhere."

Well, at least he knew what to do—it wasn't the first time it had happened.

Even before winning the World Series, Derek had been sighted by the public and the press catering to it. From the very beginning of his sports career, his combination of performance, looks, and manner had drawn attention. Now, he was the youngest player on the World Champions, and much of the luster of victory seemed to center around him. Jetermania had begun.

The first symptoms were manifest in the sports press, which had always had plenty of reason to cover the

Kid's achievements positively, and did so. Derek made the cover of *Yankees* magazine under the headline "Short and Sweet: Rookie Sensation Derek Jeter Is Electrifying the American League." Soon, the shortstop was adoringly profiled by other sports magazines— *Sports Illustrated, Sporting News, Sport*, to name a few. It was only a matter of time before the mainstream media began to circle. It quickly did.

Flush from his big success, Derek was profiled in *New York* magazine (cover), *USA Today*, *GQ* (twice— second time a cover story), numerous newspapers, and television news shows and sports shows. *People* magazine's "50 Most Beautiful People" issue in October 1997 featured an especially gorgeous shot of Jeter, which wound up pasted to thousands of bedroom walls and refrigerators. *Interview* magazine sent supermodel Veronica Webb to chat up Derek as one of the magazine's "Shooting Stars of American Sports." During the interview Jeter turned the tables and asked Webb, "You know much about baseball?" "I don't know anything about it," she admitted.

Then there was the independent, or civilian, action. Letters addressed to Derek, sometimes with only "Derek Jeter, New York Yankees" on the envelope, arrived in rising numbers. The kid from Kalamazoo was on his way to becoming the biggest mainstream superstar baseball had produced since Mickey Mantle.

How did it happen? *Why* did it happen?

Throughout this entire story, a singular, crucial fact has not yet been focused on: Derek Jeter is not only a brilliant baseball player and earnest, respectful public figure—he's also a very charming and extremely handsome young man. He's only 24, tall, with a beautifully shaded and textured complexion that sets off his green eyes very well, and has strong, attractive features that at one moment make him look like an innocent kid and at

another a sexy leading man. Powerfully built yet graceful, he wears his uniform and civilian clothes well—
which the *New York Times* quickly took advantage of
by putting Jeter on the cover of their *Men's Fashions of
the Times* supplement in March 1997.

It hasn't helped his success on the baseball field, but
it sure has off it. Baseball players are as cute or uncute
as the rest of the population but, for some reason, we
don't always think of them as seductive, glamorous figures of fantasy; it's what they can do that arouses our
interest, not how they look. That hasn't always been
true—Mickey Mantle, to take just one example, swag-
gered like a young god, arousing legions of devotees.
When both Babe Ruth and Lou Gehrig married, public
interest was enormous, not least among disheartened
women fans. The parents of some young Jeter fans
weren't immune to this: In their own adolescence, such
handsome players as Tom Seaver and Bucky Dent won
wide interest.

Jetermania is different, if not in kind, then in intensity. Maybe it's because of today's speeded-up means of
communication. Maybe it's because of an increasingly
competitive media culture, with higher financial stakes
at risk via ratings and newsstand sales. Maybe the
boundaries once separating celebrities—in movies, TV,
music, sports—are weakening. Maybe there is just
something so charming and appealing about Derek that,
to a large number of people, he appears irresistible.
Whatever, the rising tide of Jetermania hasn't crested
yet.

Writer Adrian Wojnarowski deftly captured the first
swell: ''The face of the future walks into the clubhouse
to discover clumps of correspondence stacked outside
his locker.'' This was becoming a daily fact of Derek's
life: opening, reading, responding to letters. They could
be undying declarations of love, some clearly scrawled

in an adolescent hand. They could be more seductive propositions—James Kaplan, in his incisive *New York* profile of Derek, noted one woman staring intently at the shortstop during a baseball signing and leaving him an envelope marked PERSONAL AND CONFIDENTIAL. They could enclose a Derek Jeter photo or baseball card, with a request to sign an autograph and return to the sender. ("I've been signing these since '92," Derek once shrugged casually.)

"You get the idea Jeter will convert one fan at a time," Wojnarowski continued. "Consider his talent, his charm, and it's easy to understand that his presence alone grows baseball's popularity every day. His popularity is sure to transcend the starry-eyed teenagers to the crustiest old fans." And then he added a statement that had major implications, good and bad, for the Yankees, the sport of baseball, and the love object himself: "The game has been desperate for a matinee idol."

Fortunately, the subject of all this attention was handling it very well. Amazingly well, in some opinions. *Too* well, in others.

Inevitably, Jeter is asked, over and over: How do you deal with it? It's not a question he likes to answer, and he is normally very good at answering questions. Years of feeling confident and secure about himself, and being in the public eye, have fortified him against taking acclamation too seriously. He will sometimes answer the question by sliding around it as adroitly as he steals second, saying "I'm a big fan of kids," or mentioning his own "friendliness." When asked, in effect, Why You?, he remains low key. "Kinda crazy," "Kind of overwhelming," he'll say, or explain that it has to be him and not another Yankee because he is one of the team's few bachelors.

It's clear he's given it some thought; he told *Steppin' Out* magazine, "I believe that part of the reason for all the fuss is because people don't know what nationality I am. I mean I think they know now but before people didn't know if I was Spanish, white, black, Indian. . . . So I think I can relate to a lot of people. That definitely helps.''

It is plain that while Jeter is willing to enjoy or at least put up with the attention, he knows it comes with a price. A carful of admirers shadowing Jeter after a game may be innocent; that doesn't mean they also aren't dangerous. There have been a few unnerving stories of fans who have gone too far, who can't understand that even their idol deserves some down time. *New York Post* reporter George King recounted a bizarre example of one such fan working her way from person to person in a hotel bar, looking for Yankees who would lead her to Derek; nobody would.

What Jeter is clearly more comfortable with are stories centering on his abilities as a player. When being interviewed about his career, or his skills, or his team, he is more relaxed and communicative. The real guy comes through—one who lives for the game and not the fame.

One of the very best of these profiles appeared in the February 24, 1997 issue of *Sports Illustrated*. The feature, "Short Story," profiles "the finest group of short-stops since World War II," and, on the cover, a smiling Derek pulls a loose headlock around his best-baseball-friend, Seattle Mariner Alex Rodriguez.

The piece, written by Tom Verducci, raises a particularly interesting aspect of Jeter's career: that, however remarkable his own achievement, he is not the only young, impressive shortstop to appear in major-league baseball. When he was a rookie, some articles linked him with another new New York shortstop, the Mets' Rey Ordonez; here he was also grouped with Edgar Renteria of the Florida Marlins, Alex Gonzalez of the Toronto Blue Jays, and his pal Alex Rodriguez.

"Not since 1941 have so many young shortstops arrived with this much potential," Verducci wrote, pointing out that the average shortstop of old (using the 18 currently in the Hall of Fame as a sampling) stood 5'10" and weighed 167 pounds. Like Derek, the new crop is taller, stronger, and has the potential to bring years of excitement to major league baseball. (The story featured a group portrait of the shortstops posing shirtless with gold neckchains—probably the only "beefcake" shot Jeter has ever posed for.)

The article paid particular attention to the improbably close friendship between Rodriguez and Jeter. It is unusual for players in the same position on rival teams to be so close, but, in fact, Rodriguez and Jeter had known each other for years. "Alex and I met in high school," Derek explained to *Seventeen* magazine. "We talked on the phone about whether to go to college or go with teams. Then we got really close during the rookie-development program that Major League Baseball runs. In the off-season, we play in the MTV Rock 'n' Jock softball game. We talk all the time."

Back in 1992, in Rodriguez's account, he was a senior at Miami's Westminster Christian High School, already under the same microscopic scrutiny Derek had undergone. Receiving attention from agents ("forty phone calls a night") and getting advice from "everyone in the world," Rodriguez, who knew of Jeter by reputation, suddenly knew who to reach out to for help. "I decided to call Derek, even though I didn't know him," he remembered to Bob Klapisch. "I figured he knew what I was going through."

The friendship lasted, so much so that the players put each other up at their respective apartments whenever their teams play against each other. "We get mistaken for each other all the time," Rodriguez has said. The trust that sustains the relationship was illustrated by an anecdote told by Verducci of Rodriguez asking Jeter to wake him up early for a Mariners' practice session at Yankee Stadium. Although Jeter had no practice of his own that morning, he nonetheless made sure Rodriguez made it in time: "C'mon, boy, it's time to get your butt to the ballpark," he said, whacking the sleeping Rodriguez on the hip.

"Playing against Derek makes me work that much harder. Hell, there's nothing I like better between the lines than kicking his butt," Rodriguez, perhaps not entirely seriously, has said.

Possibilities of competitive tension in the relationship don't seem to exist. Rodriguez is unquestionably the better player, and Jeter is full of praise for his friend. "He's a lot stronger than me, he hits those home runs. But I can jump better. Ask him who gets up higher on the [basketball] court. Ask him. See if he's honest."

At the time, Rodriguez responded politely: "Derek can jump," he told Klapisch. A year later, in an interview with Dan Patrick in *ESPN The Magazine*, the Mariners' shortstop, asked to reveal something about Derek Jeter "that nobody knows," was wittily blunt: "He is the absolute worst at returning phone calls. He's always late. And he's a horrible basketball player. He thinks he's got mad game, but he has no game." Presumably, this shade-throwing hasn't damaged their relationship.

Dave Campbell on ESPN's *SportsZone* wrote glowingly about the two super shortstops. "Both of them come from good families that really taught them strong values.... They're obviously going to be stars for a long while, but they treat the game right, and I can't say that for a lot of the younger players today and even many veteran players."

"Derek and I both found out we have great respect for the game," Rodriguez explains. "That's what drives us. We both want to be ambassadors for baseball, and I'm not just talking about having one great year.''

Raising the reputation of their sport really matters to these young athletes. They were on the sidelines during the bruising 1994 players' strike. They made their debuts and not only had to prove themselves (they sensed) but the viability of baseball. Their performances on and off the field have done so. This idealism has become a major part of Derek Jeter's appeal.

His determination to become an even better player (repeatedly, Derek parries compliments by insisting that until he (or any other ballplayer) has a 1.000 batting average and zero errors, there is still plenty to work on), and his refusal to relax and rake in testimonials, endorsements, and the other paraphernalia of celebrity ironically increased people's admiration—and thus his celebrity. Nothing fascinates public attention more than a star who values something greater than that attention. Greta Garbo, the movie star (that's *the* movie star) who retired in 1940 while still a young woman, spent the rest of her long life being followed about and venerated because she never gave interviews, almost never posed for photographs, and lived her own life.

Praise came to Jeter from a quarter he must value very, very much—his colleagues. During the 1997 season, fellow Yankee Mariano Duncan noted, "He came to spring training the same guy this year as he was last. A lot of guys who have big rookie years come to spring training and their attitudes are different. Not this kid. I like this kid a lot."

"You look at the younger players," manager Torre told Wojnarowski, "and you see that they all have the right attitude." This was true. Across the country a fresh generation of players was approaching the sport with a caution, media savvy and dedication that was rapidly winning back fans disenchanted with the sport after the disastrous 1994 strike.

Torre adds, with his usual frankness, "We've never done a great job of marketing our players to begin with." Other sports, he added, no doubt meaning basketball, were way ahead of his own. Basketball stars become major public figures, earning stratospheric salaries and millions more in celebrity endorsements. Not only the usual sports equipment and clothing, but all kinds of products, are sold with one beaming basketballer or another tied to the label or object. Michael Jordan's fame, and the wealth he has shrewdly reaped from it, make him one of the most celebrated humans on earth.

Against this level of achievement and exploitation, a young star like Derek Jeter is a rank beginner. Baseball players are only now beginning to earn serious consideration from product owners and advertising agencies. Set against this background, Derek hasn't done badly. He signed an endorsement with sneaker manufacturer Fila (which promptly commissioned a huge mural of the star in action, painted against the side of a building in New York's trendy SoHo), and another with Pepsi. Endorsements are lucrative, but they take work: personal appearances, photography sessions, maybe commercials. All this entails more patience, more poise before the public, more and more autographing. (Has anyone wondered how much energy baseball players—whose hands are their livelihoods—expend signing cards, programs, signs, pennants, and photos for endless lines of fans?) The money may be considerable; so is the work it demands.

The pressure to successfully manage a big career like Jeter's is intense. His agent, Casey Close of International Management Group (IMG), who played college baseball and is based in Cleveland, fields endorsement proposals for the player. In addition to Pepsi and Fila, Jeter endorsed Skippy peanut butter (his large following among kids and teens must have been a big plus in the company's eyes) and Nobody Beats the Wiz (which has recently included other Yankees like Jorge Posada and Orlando Hernandez in their commercials). And, after the 1998 World Series, Jeter, along with other Yankees, received an honor every kid good at a game dreams about: being pictured on the box of "The Breakfast of Champions," Wheaties breakfast cereal.

Perhaps his best endorsement was a print ad and commercial for the Discover card. Shown in "his" apartment, Derek explains he is expecting company, and the Discover card makes it easy to entertain. He has someone deliver the flowers, and someone else deliver the CDs he will play that evening, and (since he can't cook) someone else prepares the dinner (lobster). And, once his date arrives, what do they do? Watch highlights of the 1996 World Series.

Such endorsements add huge amounts of money and visibility to an athlete's career. In his *New York* profile of Jeter, James Kaplan interviewed sports agent Adam Katz, who gave the potential spokesman high marks for marketability—"He's extremely bright, articulate, handsome, and he's a good guy"—but then expressed reservations about some of Jeter's endorsement deals. The window of opportunity for a career, it was stressed, is brief—a few seasons, and that's it.

Endorsements have been important for Jeter, for he has not yet reached the superstar grade in terms of salary and long-term contracts. Signed by the Yankees right out of high school, he is not yet eligible for arbitration and the negotiations with other teams that could raise his Yankee compensation considerably. In 1996, he was paid $120,000 on a one-year contract. (According to *USA Today*, which reported on the negotiations, Jeter wanted more than four times that amount.) This was clearly not going to do after his amazing performance and, in his 1997 contract, the Yankees, who could have automatically re-engaged him for $150,000, offered $485,000. The final deal was for $540,000, with bonuses built-in that could have added another $25,000 to the total. He did even better in his 1998 season, earning about $750,000. With careful management, he could retire a rich man by 40, his own and his family's future secure.

It was inevitable that such an accomplished, charming person—a natural star—would attract fans. It *was* surprising when hordes of delighted fans began congregating outside stadiums and locker rooms with a heat and eagerness few earlier baseball stars had previously ignited. When Jeter plays, they rush down to the Yankee dugout to wave, or flash signs, or shout hello, or ask for autographs.

If Derek demonstrates extraordinary concentration on the playing field, some of his admirers betrayed similar determination. Jeterettes or Jetermaniacs (as they became known in the media, as dazed by this sudden phenomenon as the player himself was unruffled) began to follow his every move, and acquire every scrap of information about him they could find. Some traded info on his birthday, hometown, education, New York City residence (Upper East Side), off-season plans, favorite hangouts and restaurants, clothing stores, clubs, and bars. A few even claimed to know his underwear size. (Jeter must have greeted this news with the same reaction he usually demonstrates to questions that go too far—a startled pause followed by eye-rolling.)

At some games, dozens of teenagers buzzed in the young athlete's vicinity. This got to be a bit too much for some baseball observers. Others enjoyed this enthusiasm for Derek, hoping that it would transfer to a love of the sport, too. It has. Some Jeterettes display the same staggering, biblical knowledge of baseball and its players' skills that hardcore male fans have possessed for generations. At a recent Yankee game, three Jeter fanatics waiting for the shortstop to appear after the game so they could scream, wave, and maybe get an autograph, almost had a fight over what his 1997 season batting average was.

The center of attention handles it all so well he leaves some observers plain astonished. ''I was out at Tiger Stadium [in 1997],'' the *Kalamazoo Gazette*'s Paul Morgan recalls. ''It was a Yankee game Derek was *not* playing in—and I don't know how many teachers and students in Kalamazoo skipped school to see Derek play. He didn't, but before the game he signed autographs for as many people as humanly possible. Then he motioned other Yankee players over, and *they* joined him signing autographs! That kind of behavior is the rule with Derek, not the exception.''

James Kaplan noted the player's ability to handle admiration with dexterity, but also sensitivity. Starting with an image of the shortstop chatting after batting practice with two elderly ladies—''These are my girls,'' he says—Kaplan follows him around New York: shopping, attending a Toni Braxton-Kenny G concert at Radio City with other ballplayers (his usual companions), and then to the Coliseum, where Derek patiently signed autographs for a line of admirers so long it dwarfed those of other Yankee players and veterans. Kaplan captured the mixture of zaniness and worship in such events: Jeter, scanning the crowd beaming at him, notices a girl, maybe 12 years old, in tears. He asks the guard to bring her over. ''She can't take her eyes off Jeter, and she can't stop weeping. 'Thank you so much,' she keeps telling him.''

Derek's first response is protective: He asks her

name, and listens when, through more tears, she tells him of the hours she's waited to meet him. He tells her she should be in school. Kaplan notices Jeter's reaction: "smiling slightly, a little bemused by all this, but very cool, too." The girl stands there as Jeter signs some stuff for others and then asks her if she's all right. She replies, "I could die right now."

Researching Jeter's life story for this book has been an interesting, at times delightful, task. What makes so remarkable a person tick? How did he become the star athlete he is? What does it mean for baseball? These have been questions interesting to ask and discover answers to. But there is one crucial issue in the Derek Jeter story I cannot address alone: I am not now and have never been an adolescent female. So, in order to get at the heart of the Jeter fan phenomenon, I felt it best to bring in a panel of experts: three teenage female Jeter fans.

Colleen McCue, Heather Linderman, and Megan Sheehan are all 15 years old and live in New York state. Each is a Jetermaniac, although the term makes them roll eyes with teenage exasperation. A few days after the Yanks won the 1998 World Series, we convened in a nearby McDonald's to discuss their admiration for Derek Jeter.

Some of their comments on Jeter are familiar: "great player," "terrific guy," "It doesn't hurt that he's handsome." The tablemates giggle when Heather says this, but it's also clear that his appeal for them isn't just sexual: Each was a preteen when she first heard of the young shortstop.

Interestingly, they talk of Derek the way they would a friend, a peer. They're not overly familiar toward him, and they certainly would be awed in his presence, but there is something about Jeter they find familiar, even welcoming.

"Probably he just appeals to us because he's the

youngest on the team—he's more like a teenager than the other players," Megan states, as her comrades nod. Then she adds, "As they say, he's a kid at heart!" using a louder, ironic voice she deploys when she knows she's delivering a fierce line. (And the table erupts in laughter: friends are the best audience.)

Whatever drew them to him, it was contagious. By the start of the 1997 season, when Colleen and friends went to a game, they found themselves surrounded by other girls as smitten as they were. This was not a pleasant experience.

Each young woman has a whopping Jeter collection: baseball cards, figurines, a toy Mack truck with Derek's face on it, back issues of magazines, newspaper clippings, on-line printouts, official Yankee calendars, official Derek photographs, and, of course, caps and jerseys. No one has marketed an official line of Jeter underwear, but I suspect it would sell.

Heather's baseball card collection is incredibly cool. She has placed her cards in individual plastic holders for posterity, and can tell you where she got each one ("I spent $50 at a crafts fair for these"), which era of his career the pictures document, and which dashing image she especially favors.

Megan may not have as many cards, but she's got ones of Derek from *high school*. The teenage shortstop looks unbelievably young and cute in his Kalamazoo Maroons uniform; everyone beams at this picture. Megan's research abilities are formidable: she can reel off Jeter facts instantly, and also has his Kalamazoo address and phone number.

Megan is the only member of our panel who has had an actual close encounter with Jeter. "At Toys R Us Kids World in Elizabeth, New Jersey, on November 1, 1997, at 2:32 P.M.," Megan says with absolutely no need to refer to a calendar or notes, "I met him."

"I had just come from cross country practice, and I waited five hours on line. So, like, I was one of the last people that met him [that day]. So, I finally got up there to meet this man, and he came up to me—and my *camera* broke!" (Another photographer saved the day.) She winds up the account with "I was so excited, I nearly swooned!" Although this story has clearly been told before, her friends still follow it word for word.

Colleen McCue is the champion collector of the panel. She has a genetic advantage: Her father is a librarian. This explains the practiced skill with which she places on the table a *suitcase* of Derek Jeter material—not her entire collection—presenting her hoard with curatorial precision. For her own satisfaction, she kept a detailed record of the 1998 season on the official Yankee calendar, dates and scores of games entered in precise handwriting. Off-the-field events are included, as well. ("Strawberry's colon cancer diagnosed," fills one date.)

"I like having my own record," she explains.

"We like Derek's Turn 2 Foundation," Heather adds.

"Derek and I go way back," Megan begins, as if auditioning for *Hard Copy* or the E! Channel. Then she and her friends break up laughing.

"What really matters to us is, he's cute, he's sweet, and he's a great ballplayer!" they sum up. "And now," Megan says, all three scrutinizing their interviewer, "Tell us what *you* know. . . ."

This mass passion for the Yankee shortstop isn't limited to Colleen, Heather, and Megan's peers.

Jeter has made no bones about his pleasure at living in New York—one of the few Yankees who actually resides in the city he plays for. Although he also owns a house in Tampa, Florida, near the Yankees' training complex, Jeter still spends lots of time in Manhattan, and he has frequently been spotted there. ("Did anyone ever tell you you look like Derek Jeter?'' he was once asked by a young woman.)

Even the city's media elite behaves around him the same way his young fans do. At a reception for Jeter at the status-y hangout Moomba, local media sophistos went ga-ga over him. If Jeter has insisted dealing with the media is his biggest challenge, it must.be added his treatment by them has been remarkably kind. (Just compare it with that of other big young stars like Leonardo DiCaprio.)

Inevitably, when the shortstop first appeared on the scene, some gay Yankee fans looked at the handsome face, the built body and wondered ''Is he gay?'' Presently, the infatuation went to stage two: Rumors circulated that Jeter *is* gay. After his liaison with Carey became a news item, the rumors petered out from lack of evidence. This is a very common occurrence in today's freer gay society: a handsome man appears, you wonder, you hope—and then you get either good news (he is) or bad news (he isn't).

Gays are Jeter fans for the same reasons straights are, and they can react in as starstruck a manner as anyone. Last year a rumor spread in Chelsea, the most visible gay community in New York, that Jeter was clothes shopping in one of Eighth Avenue's fashionable men's clothing stores. Quickly a bunch of gay Jetermaniacs were peering in the windows. Was it him? What did it mean? It wasn't Jeter, but a lookalike; yet it amused an observer that so many male Jeter fans had materialized instantly to hail their idol.

Jetermania doesn't just mean fans flocking the streets or acting awestruck when meeting the shortstop of worship at a party: It means money. Jeter paraphernalia sells for more than others. Outside Yankee Stadium, a Yankee jersey with Jeter's number and name on it can sell for at least five dollars more than a ''normal'' one, or one bearing the number and name of another player. The same is true for baseball hats, laminated plaques, framed photographs, and baseball cards. Collecting baseball cards has become a multimillion-dollar avocation, and Jeter cards are now worth real money, from a single dollar (1996 Bazooka) to an amazing $1200 (1996 Certified Mirror Gold). The September 1998 magazine *Sports Cards* put Jeter on the cover and called him "The biggest star to hit New York since the Beatles." *Collecting Figures* magazine also put Derek on the cover (you don't have a head-bobbing Derek Jeter figurine?) celebrating his success and that of figurines cast in his honor.

On the Internet, there are numerous sites that, in one way or another, celebrate the shortstop. Some are quite thorough scholarly assemblies of his history, statistics, collected interviews, and photographs. Some are tender, at times embarrassing, tributes to a distant but cherished love object. Any Jeter fan should sample them—click onto a web search engine, type in the holy name, and wham—you're in Jeter Land!

What's most amazing about all this is the real calmness at the eye of the storm. New York, Derek himself explains, is a baseball town, and he left his extraordinary success at that. Baseball has tried to meet its resurgence in popularity by not leaving its young stars alone and exposed to public scrutiny. When Jeter and other young athletes are signed to the major leagues, they can get instruction from professionals in how to anticipate and negotiate the media circus that is baseball in America today. The sport has a long history of brilliant players who suffered from the plunge into notoriety. Drinking, gambling, fighting, making enemies with the press, marital troubles, extra- and postmarital troubles . . . these can all contribute to the frazzling of a great career. As fine a player as Darryl Strawberry nearly lost it all when he developed a substance abuse problem. At the same time, it's hard to destroy the affection of fans who appreciate effort and high achievement. Strawberry's sudden health crisis in the 1998 postseason almost brought New York to a standstill with concern. And such support endures: Two generations after relinquishing his position in baseball, the ailing Joe DiMaggio also received an outpouring of good will when he came down with pneumonia during that same postseason.

So the affection for Derek Jeter was clearly not simply a one-season wonder, or a skin-deep infatuation for a young, handsome guy. His fans valued him for his skills, his courtesy, his ethics, *and* his good looks.

Shirley Garzelloni was well aware of Derek's potential when she taught him in St. Augustine's—"He was just as handsome back then as he is now!"—and when asked about Jetermania, she reveals an interesting angle. "I think the reason is, there's more to beauty than just being handsome, and that's why he comes across as he does. Beauty *is* only skin deep; but there's so much more to Derek, there's so much inside him. His beauty is in his soul, in his heart. He just happens, *also*, to be handsome."

It's easy to sense that Jeter feels similarly: He doesn't make much of his looks, while not disregarding them. When faced with a wall of admirers, he doesn't preen, or shine with narcissistic pleasure. As difficult as this must be to do on a constant basis, he sees *people*, not the celebrity roadkill of adoring fans.

Still, to the athlete and his friends, it must seem a little weird: Derek Jeter, Baseball Hunk?

Fortunately, it has not driven a wedge between Jeter and his less fawned-over teammates. He can be teased about it ("Derek! Derek Jeter!" Jorge Posada falsettoed as he and Jeter were driven into that baseball event at the Coliseum) but it seems to cause his colleagues amusement and bemusement, not envy. Posada penned some witty comments on what sharing the eye of the storm with a celebrity idol can be like in a "World Series Diary" he kept for the *Journal News* in October, 1998:

"This year I got more [fan] recognition because I played a lot more. If I'm by myself, they don't know who I am on the road, but I'm always hanging around with Derek. Derek's very good, though, he's always got time for everybody. I like to be like that, but if people come up at the wrong time I'll say something, but Derek won't. He wants to say it but he won't. Derek's great with kids. He makes people happy."

Some longtime observers chuckle over this phenomenon and how the shortstop handles it. Paul Morgan: "Well, you could *almost* see that [coming] even as a teenager: he handled all the scouting stuff well, all the college stuff. . . . He was able to juggle everything and do it all well. And even that is not a put-on: it's just Derek. Still . . ." Morgan pauses for a minute, adding a distinctly Kalamazooan slant. "Back here, we all just sort of laugh when we see the Fame and Mariah things. [How people carry on] is just kind of funny."

It's poignant to hear Derek speak at length about success and its risks. He doesn't do so very often, but Peter Richmond, in a perceptive cover story on the shortstop in the September 1998 *GQ*, either caught Jeter in an expansive mood or led him into one. "It's overwhelming at times," is Derek's comment on all the adulation. What keeps Derek from getting a swelled head over all his success? The answer is a simple one: "I wouldn't be able to go home; if I want to go home, I can't do that."

"It's like everything happened so fast," he continues. "We won the World Series, the Rookie of the Year;

everything came so quick. It was like everything's been in fast-forward. It's overwhelming.''

Then, in a statement in which the man loving to play baseball suddenly realizes the boy he was is slipping away from him, he adds: ''I don't want to grow older. After you turn 21, what birthday do you look forward to? I'm not saying I don't want the future to come. But I wouldn't mind staying 23. . . . Of course, I wouldn't change anything; I have the greatest job in the world. Only one person can have it. You have shortstops on other teams—I'm not knocking other teams—but there's only one shortstop on the Yankees.''

This is what everyone must, on some level, be drawn to: the simplicity of a man who loves what he does and does it so admirably. As glamorous and sexy as he can be off the field, he is never entirely himself that way; it's while playing baseball or talking baseball that he seems the most complete—and the most fascinating.

Still, the hunk attention mounted. And it was soon noticeable wherever Jeter appeared. Even amid the universal revelry of the Yanks' 1996 World Series win, it came up. Between three and four million turned out for the ticker-tape parade in the team's honor, a lot more than showed up in 1986 for the Mets; as Darryl Strawberry put it, ''The Mets got like two million people, the Yankees had three million. The extra million were for Jeter, all those 13- and 14-year-old girls.'' Jetermania was made palpable that day by the countless signs and banners professing love and eternal devotion and the letters thrown at Derek by fans driven to screams of bliss by the briefest sight of him. His fame outside the game was becoming a story to rival his achievements within it.

As an increasingly popular public figure, Jeter was naturally expected to appear at events in New York City that regularly solicit the participation of known faces:

club and restaurant openings, benefits, parties and special events for charities, and other good causes. It was at one of these evenings, in November 1996, that he reportedly met the woman who would completely change his public persona—causing an eruption of interest from the media, an orgy of curiosity from the public . . . and a very different reaction from his longstanding fans.

Seventh Inning

Always Be My Baby

"I am not engaged. I am not getting engaged. I am not married. I am not getting married. Put that in the paper."

Derek Jeter and Mariah Carey reportedly met at a fund-raiser for the Fresh Air Fund (one of the singer's favorite charities) in November 1996. He was fresh from the Yankees' World Series win, at a point where he seemed one of New York's most popular (and sought after) residents. She was the highest-selling female pop singer of her generation, with multiplatinum CD albums and singles, married to one of the most powerful men in the music industry.

You can never tell which story of celebrity life will ignite. Publicists and consultants drag in big money helping their clients (in sports, entertainment, journalism—even politics) ensnare public attention. But, what do you do when you *don't* want that attention, when the public is fascinated by you and the person you're dating, and won't let up about it?

Much of this story skirts the constantly shifting divide between public and private life, but we do know that Derek Jeter and Mariah Carey *did* meet, and there should be no surprise at the shortstop's interest in her. Mariah Carey is, after all, of the few really sensational success stories in pop music in the '90s. Twenty-six at the time she and Jeter began keeping company, Carey's professional rise (like that of her new boyfriend's) had been rapid. Born on March 27, 1970, and raised on Long Island, her father was an aeronautical engineer, her mother an opera singer. It's immediately clear what one attraction to Derek must have been for her: their near-identical racial identity. Like Derek, she had an Irish mother, and an African-American father. "His mom is Irish and his father's black—same thing as me. I had never met anybody like that, and that's always been a big part of who I am," she told Elysa Gardner in a profile published in *In Style* magazine that may have affected her relationship with Jeter.

"A big part," is a polite way of putting the past. For, if they resembled each other in that way, Carey's own formative years were far different from her new boyfriend's. Her parents married in 1960—four years before the passage of the monumental Civil Right Act, which finally shattered the legality of racism and segregation in America; three years before Rev. Dr. Martin Luther King, Jr. led the March on Washington, which inspired enough Americans to begin to dismantle the remnants of slavery and racism that had lasted through the Civil War a century before; and several years before integration, busing, several assassinations, riots, and the explosion of black music and arts into the mainstream changed the country for good. Before Mariah's birth, the Careys moved to a succession of white neighborhoods, often enduring hostilities that tested their marriage. "They had their dogs poisoned, their cars set on fire and blown up," Carey almost matter-of-factly told *People* magazine. She knew there was a world out there that would greet the very existence of herself and her family with fear, hatred, and violence. Her older sister was beaten and taunted by other children. Carey herself was a beautiful mixture of both parents' features, with a richly colored complexion that set off her eyes and face attractively, but it led her to never be sure of who she was or where she belonged, and to be uncertain of how people would react to her.

There have been very, very few voices like Carey's in pop music. (Minnie Riperton, a Carey favorite, was one.) Carey's uniqueness lies in her ability not just to sing, but also decorate a musical line. Pop music critics are so often at sea when dealing with a voice like Carey's that they frequently mistake its size. *Vogue* breathlessly reported Carey's voice as commanding five octaves; others alleged four. (Carey has a range of three-and-a-half octaves, about standard for a coloratura soprano.)

By the time Carey met Jeter, she had created a string of unbroken hits. She became the instant idol of a generation of girls, her pretty appearance, stratospheric voice, and romantic songs of puppy love (many written in part by her) the perfect music to play again and again when you're young and believe love will be a dream come true. Peculiarly, her fan demographic even matched Derek's—like the young Madonna, Carey was worshipped by teenage girls who identified with her and copied her big hair and spiffed-up mall diva look.

We don't know how much Carey knew of Jeter when they met, but we have it on record that, months before that Fresh Air Fund benefit, he was very much aware of her. The *Bergen Record*'s Bob Klapisch was interviewing Derek in April 1996 while the Yankees were down in Arlington, Texas playing against the Texas Rangers. Bored by a game postponement, reporter and subject were running down the list of basic questions, when suddenly, as Klapisch puts it, "the conversation road led Jeter to a topic that raised his blood pressure." Klapisch reports the scene:

Teammate Dion James happens by, and says "Jeet, I'll get that Mariah Carey tape back to you soon."

"Mariah? Man, don't be messing with my girl," Derek answers, "beaming," Klapisch notices.

Yankee Jim Leyritz laughs and says "Your girl, Jeet?"

"'Yup, gonna marry her,' Jeter said matter-of-factly."

Leyritz reminds his teammate of the reality: that Carey is already married, and her husband is a music industry bigwig. "Think of all those millions," he adds.

Klapisch watches Jeter shake his head. He responds, "So what? He's old. Wait till she finds out I'm out there."

"The room broke up in laughter," Klapisch continues, "although Jeter was still half-serious. Carey will learn, at least if she's a baseball fan."

Okay—stop a second and take another look at that exchange. Then remember that the speaker bragging about his future conquest is a 21-year-old embarking on the biggest season of his life. Now it sounds less like a cocky exchange and more like a boy's wish turned into a boast. If anything, what later transpired between Derek Jeter and Mariah Carey was a fluke (or a happy accident of fate) rather than another carefully executed fulfillment of one of Derek's dreams.

We don't know if Carey is (maybe now *was*) a baseball fan, but we do know two things: She and Derek Jeter supposedly met in November 1996. A month later, Carey was said to be spending far less time in her Bedford, New York, matrimonial palace. Six months later, in May 1997, the Mottolas announced their separation.

Did Derek play a role in all this? We don't know. Rumors began to surface almost at once linking the singer and the shortstop, but they were never substantiated. And it must also be said that there had been rumors about the state of the Mottola-Carey marriage before Mariah's meeting with Derek, even before the young shortstop's comments to Klapisch in April 1996. Carey marrying a much older, very powerful man who masterminded some of her success probably helped inspire the caustic, sometimes downright mean, press she has steadily received.

If she thought life had been a balancing act before—satisfying her young, adoring, mostly teenage fans on one hand, and an older, more skeptical music industry and press on the other—Mariah Carey was about to discover that being linked to the young star of the New York Yankees would not be another Cinderella story. Instead, both were about to begin a tabloid nightmare.

Jeter had heretofore done an amazing job of keeping his social life to himself. There were a few mentions of a sweetheart in Kalamazoo and, then, once he established himself in New York, some dates that didn't develop into anything. "Do you have a girlfriend?" one reporter asked him, and he shook his head and answered "I need one. I need some help." This young man, who handled public attention very well, but also valued his privacy once he stepped off the ballfield, was about to discover how fragile "privacy," for a famous person, can be.

In 1998, Carey was noticed attending Yankees spring training and, as her marriage to Mottola approached its end, keeping her relationship with Jeter a secret became impossible. So, when the stories (in print, on the air, on the web, in general talk) began slinging the dirt on the couple, with marriage speculations included in the mix, Derek decided to speak out. Talking to Jack Connell of the Hartford *Courant*, he was direct and firm, the way he usually is:

"I am not engaged. I am not getting engaged. I am not married. I am not getting married." He then added, betraying, perhaps, his feelings about the whole brouhaha, "Put that in the paper."

Well, he couldn't have been *totally* surprised at the public curiosity. He had already endured a year of more press than some athletes get in a lifetime, all of which was sympathetic, even rose-colored. From the media, he had little to fear other than their continued interest in him. But now, he had made a move that not only captured more attention, but fused his own allure to that of another star's: he was dating the top-selling female singer of the decade—a woman who was an even bigger star in her world than he was in his. One star out in the night, and the street they're traveling sparks with camera flashes. Two stars together, the paparazzi and TV crews brighten up the neighborhood. Two young, handsome stars *dating*, and the city of media goes nuclear.

On March 7, the *Daily News* reported on several Derek-Mariah sightings amid spring training. Suddenly, what they wore and how they styled their hair that day were pertinent details for public consumption, as well as where they ate and how they behaved. Expert testimony was elicited—a waiter who served them thought they looked "lovey-dovey" together. The *News* reporter was only one of a gathering army of representatives, some from venues not normally known for covering sports. Now, Jeter was not just an athlete, but a celebrity date, and the tabloids (print and television), once a new subject is sighted in their viewfinders, pursues the latest chosen one relentlessly. Derek's denials only quickened the demand for more news of the couple.

If Jeter sometimes looked as if he were dodging bullets, the other person in the spotlight coped with outward calm. Maybe it was because of their different careers. Carey, as a pop star, *must* make her private life part of the act with which she attracts and entertains her public. Derek can polish off a great game and expect to go home, or out, and not have to keep playing The Star. Entertainers are not athletes, however; the demands made of them are different. We expect them *never* to take off the mask. Their homes and wardrobes and sex lives are considered accessories to the singing or acting they do. There is an entire industry that chronicles their comings and goings, that helps create and sustain the public fantasy that becomes Mariah Carey or Leonardo DiCaprio or Calista Flockhart or Tom Cruise. There is another part of that same industry that flourishes by challenging the fantasy, backing the star into a corner and ripping off the mask—showing the crowd of fans that their idol is merely human, after all. Flinching too much in the face of such scrutiny, or showing undue signs of wear or stress, can torpedo a career, no matter how talented the artist really is.

Carey had been dealing with this dilemma since she became a recording artist. She couldn't dress the way she always wanted, because a daring or more adult look (darker nail polish or lipstick, even) might clash with the image of Mariah Carey flourishing in her fans' imaginations. As a star and the wife of a rich and powerful music executive, Carey was watched and handled and followed by people representing her record company's interests—Carey was not only a person, she was a property. In a profile of the singer that ran in *Vogue*, Carey's limo was chased down because the singer and *Vogue's* Vicki Woods climbed into Carey's limousine—unchaperoned! Into the limo leapt a Sony Records representative, whose plans to monitor (and perhaps censor) the interview were thwarted when Carey put up a privacy screen, soundproofing their talk.

Derek certainly had public pressures to deal with—but on this level? Doubtful. But in becoming involved (however involved) with Mariah Carey, he was already wedding himself to the frenzy she had to negotiate daily. Avid interest was fed by a media delighted two such wildly popular stars from different fields should come together. Star romances are a staple of celebrity lore: Joe DiMaggio and Marilyn Monroe were just one (close) example. As if negotiating a budding relationship wasn't tough enough, Carey and Jeter now had to do so under the scrutiny—and commentary—of a nation of inquisitive eyes.

"It's bad enough when one public person is involved," Carey complained. "But with two, it's really hard to have something to yourself." Ordinary activities romantic couples could indulge in—dinner at a restaurant, dancing—become obstacle courses for couples bearing famous faces. It's easy to say that this gauntlet-running is a small price to pay for millions of dollars and widespread adulation, but that easiness evaporates when you can't even meet your girlfriend anywhere in Manhattan without wondering who saw you, who may now be watching you, and what the fallout from this encounter will be.

Most of the public was no doubt pleased their hero had fallen into company with such a talented, lovely person.

But the Carey-Jeter stories provoked real repercussions. The New York Yankees are widely respected, even idolized—but Jeter is *loved*. It isn't just that women find him handsome: There is something about Jeter that causes them to lose their marbles in adulation. If the athlete had any doubts on this issue, they were put to rest during the parade saluting the Yanks after the 1996 World Series, when women in the crowd spotted Jeter, and turned into raving acolytes. "DEREK! DE-REK!" they screamed en masse, causing even policemen holding back the crowd to cover their ears. They had to uncover them fast, as some Jeter admirers threw themselves against anything in their way, flying like kamikazes across the air separating them from their idol. Those that didn't hurl themselves at the float carrying

Jeter (who, it must be said, kept smiling and waving cheerfully in the midst of a scene that would have sent weaker souls fleeing in panic) stood and waved, or bounced up and down, or screamed "I LOVE YOU!" at the top of their lungs. "I don't know what happened to us," a normally calm secretary admitted later. "We saw the Yankee floats, and we saw Derek waving, and he flashed us that smile—my God, that *smile*—and every one of us completely lost it. Half the women on my floor were so exhausted afterwards, they skipped work and just went home. It was pure insanity. We loved it."

Stars fulfill dreams, and not only their own. Admirers look to them for behavior to emulate, looks to appropriate, achievements to feel vicariously proud of. However, the admiration can get out of hand. "The trouble with fame is, it goes to the heads of people who aren't famous," opera star Maria Callas, whose public image was totally destroyed by an envious media, declared with typical insight. Derek Jeter's fame is rewarding, but also a burden. He has to be aware that, in the clamor of his hugely successful, rewarding life, a bewitched public will demand high job performance and personal integrity. And he must certainly know that there are legions of young women and girls who have active imaginations, in which he plays a prominent role.

In such a situation, it is all but impossible for Jeter and Carey to behave like a normal couple. Celebrities quickly learn to cope with inordinate public attention.

Fortunately, Jeter will probably not develop symptoms of celebritymania, as other popular public figures do. He has never trashed a room in a hotel (like Johnny Depp), shown up at an autograph signing in bridal satin (like Dennis Rodman), or gotten married while intoxicated (you know who)—and never will. The discipline and support of Jeter's rearing have made his success possible, and given him the ability to handle it well.

In the frenzy of renown, sometimes just *thinking* you are within breathing distance of a luminary is enough to cause a commotion. Derek and Mariah began being spotted all over the place by thrilled, frustrated, or venomous fans. They spirited away for an amorous weekend somewhere and were ''seen.'' Presently, it would be revealed it couldn't have been them—Jeter was playing for the Yanks that weekend, in another part of the country, and no, no one had seen Carey at the stadium or with the player afterward. But, just as one story was deflated, another began. The couple became a Celebrity Mirage that the faithful—and the media—sighted again and again.

What the reality of the relationship was is pretty much impossible for us to judge. We simply don't know much about what went on between Mariah Carey and Derek Jeter. The public knowledge of their affair, or liaison, or dating (we don't even know which it was) can be watered down to a few glimpses, a clutch of denials or avowals, and a final, terse statement of dissolution. And, anyway, what could they tell us if they chose to? We met. We went out. We danced. We ate. We bought each other presents. We did it (or we didn't do it). We agreed on some things. We disagreed on others. We broke up.

What is really interesting about this story is the reaction it inspired in others. For as soon as the rumors linking the Yankee shortstop to the CBS siren hit the papers, TV shows, the E! Channel, and the Internet, from across the land could be heard a collective squawk of horror from millions of (primarily female) throats. Suddenly, their idol, their Derek, was no longer theirs, but *hers*. Fantasy lives choked and died horrible deaths all over the place as the reality of a Derek in someone else's arms provoked fury.

As if the romantic imagination isn't potentially treacherous enough, sometimes the press getting things wrong fed the obsession with the couple. Fans were shocked, then skeptical, of reports of the Yankee and the Sony music siren taking in the sights at a well-known strip bar. ("Derek would *never* behave like *that*!" more than one declared.) Derek had had to clear the air about such stories before: after finishing up the 1997 post-season (the Yanks didn't make it to the World Series that year), the team partied to cheer themselves up. Soon news stories claimed the after-hours revel had been a wild one, with strippers and other carryings-on. The Yankee organization was said to be embarrassed, but Jeter was having none of it.

"That was another made up story!" he insisted in a long, generous interview with *Steppin' Out* magazine (which plastered an insert portrait of Carey on a cover featuring Jeter). The team was hanging out in a bar that became crowded with other people. "But the papers made it sound like we were there with a bunch of strippers and that people were making out in corners of the bar. I mean I'm not denying that there were strippers at the party but they were dressed like my mom dresses. Like a normal person. I think the whole thing made us look bad but the team knows what really happened and what the truth is."

At times, answering the press attention and allegations must have seemed like a losing battle to him. "I know people who read the papers are going to believe what they read. There's nothing I can do about that."

This wasn't a completely new experience, either. Earlier, he had been alleged to be dating supermodel Tyra Banks. Banks and Jeter are both IMG clients, and they were seated next to each other at a New York Knicks game. Other celebrities would have thought little of the misperception, maybe even appreciated the press attention. But Jeter carefully, even laboriously corrected the reports: "The truth was the only time I ever saw Tyra Banks was at that basketball game."

Jeter doesn't come from a celebrity-based culture. His values are based on achievements in a sport with a short but fiercely cherished history. When confronted with attention he considers unwarranted, rumors that aren't true, he doesn't go along—he wants to speak the truth, and be heard, and believed. This situation with Carey couldn't have been easy to handle. It wasn't much easier for those who covered him before Mariah Carey whisked into his life. Suddenly baseball's fine young hero was Hunk of the Month. An aghast *Yankees* magazine column deplored the entire spectacle, slightly undercutting its argument with the tabloidy headline LET'S NOT GET CAREYED AWAY. (And even sports devotees gossip: "What have *you* found out?" a writer on Jeter was asked again and again, before anything else.)

A closer view of the affair comes from a source who knows Jeter well, and watched him weather the rumor storm of early 1998. "I don't think Derek liked it," the observer says. "I thought I saw in him, for the first time, a little self-consciousness. It's the only time I sensed him a *bit* out-of-kilter." This person witnessed firsthand how smoothly Jeter usually handled the attention and admiration he receives: "Most guys would go bananas. These women, they get so excited when Derek's around. But he really handles it so well. If you didn't see it, you wouldn't believe it."

And, exactly, what was going on? Jeter's reaction, as read by this observer, was strong, and surprising. "Derek can handle publicity. But he didn't like the idea the media was setting him up with this girl. I think he thought their attitudes were a little childish."

This account challenges most perceptions of the Carey-Jeter liaison. Maybe Jeter was uncomfortable in part because there really wasn't much there. Until both parties speak up about it (don't hold your breath) we'll simply never know. And Jeter's silence reminds of us something else: that real people are involved here, not "celebrities." All the scrutiny was clearly making things difficult. "It didn't happen," Jeter firmly replied when *GQ*'s Peter Richmond asked about a story that placed the couple at a strip joint; Jeter then added, "a cloud of anger shadowing his face, '*Of course* it didn't happen.' " That *Of course* admits a great deal: how trying it is to live under a microscope, to enjoy the normal pleasures of life—romance, privacy, freedom—when your every move is a media event, and how frustrating it must be to know you're losing control of how people know you and judge you. He tried to keep the story to his career: "They can write what they want but I am just talking about baseball."

The Mariah mania (as opposed to the Jetermania, which, in two seasons, everybody seemed to have adjusted to splendidly) went as far as it could go: It intruded on his game. More than one observer suggested baseball was a refuge for Jeter, a guaranteed magic time. Now that sanctuary was threatened by fans holding signs inscribed DEREK & MARIAH, a big heart connecting the two names. When the love object herself appeared at a game, bleachers and boxes hummed with excitement, like hives of innuendo. And sometimes things got *really* nasty in the ballpark. In May 1998, when the Yanks played in Chicago, whenever Jeter stepped up to the plate the stadium loudspeakers blasted not "We Are the Champions" or "We Will Rock You," but "Always Be My Baby," one of Mariah Carey's hits. How can anyone hit a homer with his girlfriend's voice blasting through the stadium, to the accompaniment of thousands of giggling onlookers?

It didn't intimidate him, at least not obviously. "They

were pulling them out of the archives!'' Derek commented after that incident, perhaps wondering how closely people would be scrutinizing future Mariah Carey lyrics. ''That got old after a while.'' Fortunately, he could dismiss this situation easily: the Yanks whammed Chicago that day, 7-5. (Any effect this incident had on Chicago sales of Carey's records has not been recorded.)

All spring, the tabloids had a field day with the story, covering the affair despite a near-total dearth of information. Disconsolate Jeter fans who, perhaps, had been counting the years until they'd be old enough to win the shortstop for themselves, no doubt reacted to some of the din by scanning their Jeter scrapbooks, perhaps finding such quotes from their idol as ''You can't find love. . . . Love finds you,'' balm for their disappointment.

But then, with supreme ill-timing, right after the Mottolas' marriage officially ended in the spring of 1998, the Derek and Mariah thing got ugly. A former driver for Carey, Franco D'Onofrio, surfaced. *LIMO SUIT MIGHT AIR MARIAH'S DIRTY LINEN*, cried the *New York Post* on June 8. ''The steamy details of Mariah Carey and Derek Jeter's hot romance could be aired in public if a lawsuit from the pop diva's former limo driver makes it to a courtroom,'' the lead ran. The story reported D'Onofrio as preparing to file papers alleging Carey owed him thousands in fees.

Other dailies instantly picked this up. So did the Associated Press. The next day, Carey and her people came out swinging, to the same *Post* reporter (Jeane MacIntosh) who had broken the story in the first place. A staffer in Carey's camp declared ''It's obvious this is about money and headlines,'' and the singer herself hardly remained silent.

Even if none of these stories were true (and, according to *Newsday*, an attorney for the complaining chauffer did damage control, claiming his client ''never made those statements . . . he wouldn't say such things for obvious business reasons"), they made Jeter, normally prized for his fresh-faced, good-boy manner, seem a little . . . well, racier. It was as if his fans suddenly realized that, beyond the sweet young man they prized, there was also a normal adult male who had his own personal, romantic, even sexual, life. This revelation, instead of deterring Jeter's admirers, only seemed to create more of them. For within weeks of Jeter and Carey keeping company, the athlete's popularity went into overdrive. (In November 1998, D'Onofrio's suit against Carey was dismissed.)

There were already *other* stories circulating that even the Yankees were concerned about their shortstop's love life. There was a story that Jeter, normally affable when joshed about one thing or another by his teammates, made it clear that kidding about Carey was off-limits. There was a rumor George Steinbrenner himself had asked Jeter about the situation, advising him to "keep a lower profile" with Carey. She fielded this one. "What?" she responded, again, to the *Post*. "I'm just a singer, not some magical baseball genie who can make or break someone's game."

When *Steppin' Out* claimed that Jeter's own teammates "were quoted as saying they were concerned when they heard that you and Mariah Carey were dating again because they felt it affected your concentration," you can all but hear the guy sighing, gritting his teeth, and squaring his shoulders.

"I don't think any of my teammates said that," he responds, "but that's a whole 'nother thing. Either way, they don't have to worry about me. See, concentration would never be a problem because I have my priorities straight. My main goal is to do well at baseball. And I let nothing get in the way of that."

Here was a blunt statement of principle everyone

could understand. *My main goal is to do well at base-ball.* We don't know if actions taken subsequent to those chauffer stories were inspired by letting nothing "get in the way of that," but the congruence is provocative.

Right after those rumors ran in the tabloids, *In Style* published a cover story featuring Mariah Carey. Amid shots of her new, post-Mottola Manhattan home, photos of the pop diva posing surrounded by her wardrobe and shoes and giggling in her bubblebath, ran a long, positive profile in which she spoke with more frankness than ever before of the Jeter Situation. The author cites as "an anomaly in Carey's jacket collection" a blue New York Yankees jacket. "I went to a game the other day and I got cold, so I bought one," Carey says "coyly." "Without much pressing," *In Style*'s Elysa Gardner continues, "she tells the real story: The rumors that she is dating Derek Jeter are true." She talks about celebrity and public exposure, and of having an Easter party in the new apartment, the guests including "some of the people we talked about before," obviously meaning Derek. Her last quote in the interview was "Now I'm just trying to enjoy my life."

Just as *In Style* was reaching newsstands and subscribers' mailboxes, the whole story seemed to put a halt to itself. On June 12 both the *Post* and *News* led with fresh news: DEREK AND MARIAH STRIKE OUT; MARIAH AND JETER CALL IT QUITS ON ROMANCE. "Just when it looked like the singer and the Yankee shortstop were becoming New York's sweethearts, their romance has wilted under the media glare," reported *News* gossip columnists Rush and Molloy. Carey publicist Berger was quoted as saying "They're cooling off," adding "The public scrutiny became more than they can take."

"They have decided to take a step back," Berger informed the *Post*. "The media pressure got to them.

The decision was mutual. The scrutiny was just too much, on both sides.''

Rush and Molloy got off a good line when they claimed ''Jeter and Carey spent most of their relationship denying they had a relationship.'' They hastened to add that Berger stated Carey was seeing no one, but that Jeter was allegedly spotted the weekend before at Wax, a SoHo club, ''ignoring [pitcher] Hideki Irabu and other teammates and cozying up to a stunning blonde, with whom he left.''

Did the lawsuit threat have anything to do with the decision? No, said Berger. But the climate of unrelenting scrutiny, fed in part by the lawsuit, possibly did.

From all over the place, Jeter fans could be heard sighing in relief. Interestingly, almost every Jetermaniac queried took for granted it was *Jeter* who ended the relationship, despite public statements that the decision was mutual. ''We love Derek now that he got rid of Mariah!'' a young female fan shouted during the 1998 Victory Parade on lower Broadway; her surrounding friends met this remark with a roar of agreement. It was pretty clear which member of the former couple was receiving most of the negative feelings aroused over the affair.

The final public view we have of the couple together came at a birthday party for Sean ''Puffy'' Combs at the new, swanky Cipriani Wall Street on the evening of November 4, 1998. Thousands of guests, the famous, the notorious, and the ambitious, fought to get past security into the loud, packed party. Despite the plethora of names and faces, the story of the night (aside from the utter chaos of the event) concerned Derek and Mariah. More than four months had passed since the announcement of their ''tak[ing] a step back.'' They were at the party, if not together. She was on the arm of supermodel Marcus Schenkenberg; Jeter attended, as he often does such events, with several buddies. What happened next was a lead story in the gossip pages the next day.

At first, it sounds like a scene from a music video. As the *News* related, around 1:00 A.M. Carey, date in tow, saw Jeter in the crowd and approached him. At first she poked him in the chest and tickled his sides. The only response she got from Derek was polite chit chat. Then, she escalated offense, whispering in his ear and putting her arms around him. A photo taken at the event shows Jeter looking a bit awkward and Carey, her face an inch from his, appearing absolutely smitten.

Finally, with Schenkenberg still waiting beside her and Carey continuing, Jeter seemed to have had enough. "You're crazy," the *News'* Mitchell Fink quotes Jeter as saying to his former girlfriend. "You're crazy. Stop pushing me." Then he turned his back on her. Carey, described as reluctant, moved on with her date, leaving the party not long after.

It might have started as a scene from a music video, but it turned into a celebrity head-on. Whatever was between them didn't seem to end with the perfect resolution of art, but the mess of gossip and the jumble of real life.

Almost no Jeter watchers, questioned for a reaction to this event, found any humor in the report. Instead, it left behind a bittersweet, even bad taste. "Actually, it makes me feel sad for both of them," one of his biggest fans said.

Eighth Inning

Simply the Best

"I don't think there's a person in the world who's been more spoiled than I've been."

For a season that would become not just victorious but historic, Derek Jeter and the New York Yankees began 1998 somewhat tentatively. Nineteen ninety-seven had been another fine year for the shortstop and his team, but it ended abruptly when the Yankees, against expectations, didn't ride the postseason all the way. Beaten by the Cleveland Indians in the American League's best-of-five division series, they returned to New York as baffled as their fans. One look at Derek as the Yanks trotted off the field said it all: no dream this year.

If in 1998 Jeter had to perform with giggles about Mariah Carey circling him, in 1997 he battled, bizarrely, low expectations. A sophomore slump was predicted for him and, even though he finished the season well, with a .291 average and 70 runs batted in, worries about his long-term performance as a Yankee were heard. For someone as dedicated to always improving as he is, this dust storm of speculation couldn't have been easy to tolerate, or ignore.

By the time 1998 spring training began (despite the distraction of Mariah on the sidelines in Tampa), the worries and disappointments of 1997 had been put in perspective. From the very beginning of the new season, team members, management, and onlookers sensed this would be no ordinary year. Something amazing was going to happen in baseball in 1998, and it had *Yankees* written all over it.

We all know how this wondrous season ended, but have we already forgotten how shockingly it began? When the team blew three games right away, and seemed lost on the field, and George Steinbrenner's outrage actually seemed justified, and even Joe Torre looked beleaguered? In New York, failure is never good, but when it's spectacular at least it gives people something to talk about, and the Yankees-as-Losers became a ghastly conversation piece. Rumors even spread that Torre's managing career, looked upon by much of the public as sacred, was in jeopardy.

Maybe they all ate lousy food during spring training, or just needed to feel the urge to prevail again. Whatever, the Yankees began winning, and once they started, they couldn't seem to stop. The rest of the season became an exhausting series of triumphs and, by May, Yankee fans were laying plans for securing tickets for the World Series. In its June 2nd issue, *ESPN The Magazine* declared "It's over," about the American League race. The only question seemed to be, who would they ultimately play against—and beat?

A season this spectacular must have been a deliverance for Derek. All year his private life heated airwaves and sold newspapers, but nobody could stop him on the ballfield. He has always had the gift of responding well to his surroundings, and he was surrounded by a team not of solo champions, but an ensemble that played together better than perhaps any other in the history of baseball. It wasn't a season of personal bests (although Jeter's stats were his finest yet with the Yanks), but of a collective effort that almost never flagged. The sheer determination and expertise of the New York Yankees in 1998 was awesome.

Derek's own playing grew in assurance and finish. Throughout the season, he would rally his team at bat when they were behind, and close in on balls flying his way like heatseeking missiles. His trademark single-motion delivery—racing to a ball, catching it, then throwing it to Chuck Knoblauch at second or Tino Martinez on first in one unbelievably fluid motion—became more dazzling as the weeks, and the wins, progressed. His excellence was rewarded by his first-ever play in an All-Star game and his third-place ranking in the voting for MVP in the American League.

It wasn't a season without problems. Early in June, the ever-reliable Derek wound up, of all places, back in the minors! During a fifth inning swing Jeter strained an abdominal muscle while checking his swing on a 3-1 pitch. He started, and Joe Torre, immediately sensing something amiss, hurried to home plate. Jeter insisted he could continue. He trickled a grounder to second base on the very next swing, but he was obviously hurt and Torre removed him from the game, placing him on the dreaded disabled list.

Not playing baseball is a reality Derek Jeter probably loathes more than any other. After the game, he met Torre in the parking lot and, as the manager related to Mark J. Czerwinski, said "I'll play tomorrow," to which his boss replied "Maybe not."

It was maybe not for 15 days. He had never been on the DL before, never missed a Yankee game because of injuries. Now he was forced to rest, and he clearly didn't like it. "It's frustrating," Derek admitted to writer Ken Davidoff. "[But] I don't want to be stupid and risk injuring it more severely." He had joked in the past that if it weren't for Torre thwarting his attempts, he'd one day have an attendance record to rival Cal Ripken's. But this enforced absence was no joke.

In just over two weeks he was back, after a single minor-league game convinced the Yankees his abs were healed. Derek rejoined the Yankees as they played a season for the ages.

When the regular season was over, the Yankees had won 114 games (with 48 losses), making them the second-most-winning season team in baseball history. (The 1906 Chicago Cubs beat this year's Yanks by two games—116–36—but they lost the 1906 Series.) They became the highest single-season winners in their league, and the biggest winners since teams began playing a 162-game schedule. They smacked 207 home runs, the second highest in Yankee history. (Derek was one of the eight Yankees who hit at least 15 homers in the season.)

Most important, the team's heroic playing buried the lingering ghosts of the 1994 baseball strike. With the Yankees outperforming everyone and Mark McGwire and Sammy Sosa dueling to break the single season home-run records of two of the greatest Yankees (Babe Ruth and Roger Maris), it was a miraculous time for baseball. For young people, it was a season they would always remember; for older fans, a happy reminder of how magical and perfect baseball still could be. By the time the Yankees steamrollered into the playoffs, with milestones like David Wells's pitching a perfect game (against the Minnesota Twins on May 17), and David Cone notching 20 wins in a single season, absolute triumph seemed certain.

They seemed to dash through the division series against the Texas Rangers, allowing them only one run (despite the most potent lineup in the AL) in three games, as if this division championship was just something to get out of the way before running through the pennant and World Series. Yankee watchers, with two rounds of the playoffs left to go, were already exhausted with admiration.

Nothing ever comes as easily as it should, though, and the team—and one of its most beloved players—was about to be hit hard.

Earlier in the summer, Darryl Strawberry had experienced some intestinal problems. Just before the closing rounds in their division title championship against the Rangers, test results were in: Strawberry had a walnut-sized malignant tumor on his colon.

Although the initial prognosis was good—a young man who had survived substance-abuse problems and other personal and professional trials, Strawberry had worked hard to put his life back on track, and was in otherwise fine health—the news devastated his teammates. Notified by their manager in the locker room, they spent time together, absorbing the news through talk and prayer. (Some players brought out their Bibles.) The team practice the day they heard the news was said to be the quietest, most subdued ever.

Beyond the locker room, the city that had seen Strawberry get clobbered by misfortune before, and doggedly get up to keep pitching, greeted the news the same way. Strawberry received masses of prayers, messages, flowers, and good wishes. The surgery, on Saturday, October 3, went well. Although tests revealed minor cancer growths beyond the tumor, doctors were hopeful a course of chemotherapy would ensure the player's recovery—and a return to the Yankees.

Strawberry, missing the team as much as they missed him, had videotaped a message for them two days before his surgery: "Go get 'em tonight, guys." Sure enough, the Yankees charged through their game with the Texas Rangers, defeating them 4-0. They faced their first game against the Cleveland Indians, who had unexpectedly finessed them the year before, for the American League pennant title.

The day after Strawberry's operation, Jeter, as well as manager Torre, Dave Cone, Andy Pettite, Chili Davis, Tim Raines, and Tino Martinez, visited him in the hospital, as did George Steinbrenner. "We're all concerned about him," Cone, one of the most thoughtful and eloquent members of the team, told Jack Curry at the *New York Times*. "We want to see how he's doing. It will be nice to see him face to face and tell him how much we care." Cone and the others brought a present for their colleague—a Yankee cap embroidered with the number 39, Strawberry's team number. All the Yankees had 39s sewn onto their own caps, and soon the whole city suddenly seemed full of number 39s. (Even Cleveland Indians and San Diego Padres teammates—and their fans—adopted the gesture.)

Misfortune didn't threaten the glow of achievement in the clubhouse; it only clarified it. This was a game, and games matter, but other things—family, health, love—matter more. As tragedy sometimes does, it united not only the team but their fans. "Doing it for Darryl" became the slogan of the postseason.

Whatever the motivations, the Yankees certainly did it, for Darryl, and themselves. In the opening game of the American League Championship Series, before a sold-out Yankee Stadium, the Indians got trounced, with five runs scored in the first inning alone (and against pitcher Jared Wright, who had owned the Yankees in last season's playoffs). Derek made one of his amazing, airborne plays in the fourth inning, when Indian Travis Fryman hit a grounder into left field. Soaring upwards, the shortstop did a backhand catch and then, still in mid-air, threw the ball to first, recording the out. The stadium crowd reacted as it often does to Jeter plays—a gasp followed by a roar of approval and thousands of heads shaking in amazement.

In his third season with the team, the shortstop seemed to be getting stronger, faster, surer, game after game. Spectators leaned forward excitedly as soon as the ball struck from whichever opposing team soared or rolled in Jeter's direction: What was he gonna do *now?* Derek seemed to be finding new ways to streamline his performance, rushing forward or backward to get the ball with longer, faster steps, seeming to be hurling the ball for an out before he had actually gotten it in his glove. It all looked not only powerful and practiced, but graceful, almost expressive. "God, he's *more* wonderful!" one Yankee fan said to another, watching that play in Game 1 of the pennant series.

Although more experienced players and coaches had cautioned against these virtuoso leaps and midair plays, Jeter only improved doing them. They never appeared show-offy, full of the flash that other players sometimes add to gain applause or media approval. When Derek Jeter seems to blast off into midair, you know that his instincts and flawlessly trained reflexes send that muscular yet elegant body flying—because every fiber of him wants, more than anything, to complete each play.

Game 1 of the ALCS was a 7-2 win for the Yanks that seemed characteristic of their season-sweeping tactics. But Game 2 became infamous overnight when, after a 12-inning bruiser of a game with a one-all score, Indian Travis Fryman bunted and ran toward first on the grass. Tino Martinez threw to second baseman Chuck Knoblauch, but the ball hit Fryman in the back and bounced to the infield dirt. The ball was still in play, but Knoblauch didn't even seem to notice, arguing with the umpire over Fryman's interference. Meanwhile, the stadium, the Yankees, and millions of watchers screamed "GET THE BALL!" at Knoblauch, but it was too late.

Cleveland scored, Fryman reached third, and the Indians finished off the Yanks 4-1.

The fury that nuked Knoblauch was unanimous. BLAUCHHEAD ran one scornful headline. The poor guy faced an incensed New York the next morning, looking miserable, uttering apologies accepted by no one, especially when the Yankees lost the next game 6-1 and their glorious season threatened to evaporate in the October chill.

Salvation arrived in Game 4 at the hands of Orlando "El Duque" Hernandez, one of the success stories of the season. A recent refugee from Cuba, he demonstrated a coolness in the face of adversity that helped him lead the way in vanquishing the Indians, 4-0. While the Indians played hard in the next two games, they never managed to beat the Yanks again. Game 5 went to the Bombers, 5-3, and Game 6, thanks to a late rally by Jeter and others, completed the rout, 9-5. The Yankees were ready to play their second World Series in three years.

That final ALCS game had been full of excitement. If the Yankees' batters had been underperforming in the first rounds of the postseason, they now came out swinging, as if to stop talk of a slump once and for all. Jeter hit a two-run triple in Game 6 that proved decisive in ensuring a victory. Once again, this remarkable ensemble seemed to re-energize not only themselves but each other.

If the clinching game is always a blur of anxiety, the pace picks up once the team has won. In an instant, the Yankee dugout and locker room were filled with excited players, relatives, friends, Yankee personnel, and reporters. As the players whooped and laughed through the traditional victory celebration of spraying each other with bottles of champagne, they were surprised by the appearance of their owner, George Steinbrenner. When the team clinched victories in the American League East and division competitions earlier, the Boss had discreetly stayed away as everyone else got doused. But now, here he was, looking more emotional and excited than usual, expressing his enthusiasm to reporters.

Behind the ring of reporters a voice suddenly called "Oh, Boss Man . . ." and then "Hold on! Somebody's dry around here," and, in a flash, Derek leaned over the reporters, a cigar in his mouth and an entire open bottle of champagne in the hand that had helped clinch the pennant. A gasp went up from the reporters as he deftly emptied the bottle of champagne onto The Boss's very neat, omnipotent head. Amid onlooker "Ooooooooohhs," a laughing Jeter yelled, "I got him!" as his team's owner—fortunately—spluttered, gaped, and laughed a little.

Are you getting spoiled? Jeter was asked by reporters as corks popped and champagne flew in everyone's faces. Their reply was a sheepish grin and "I'm used to this. I really don't know anything else. Is that getting spoiled?

"In '96, everything was new to me. Everything happened so fast to me and before you knew it, I was in the World Series.

"We have so many ways to win."

Jeter's hitting in the series had been only 3-for-20, so his hits in Game 6 went a long way to restate his power at bat. The final one was especially thrilling, because as he put it later "I hadn't hit a ball in the air since the second game." This one was airborne and then some: It seemed ready to go over the fence. Indians outfielder Manny Ramirez literally climbed the back wall to catch it, but it landed just below him, making him scramble for it as Jeter sped to third and two runs ran home, putting the Yankees ahead again. When Bernie Williams's third hit of the game sent Jeter in, fans in the stands were already lining up for World Series tickets.

This was going to be an easy World Series win, the Yankees' admirers debated—or wasn't it?

"I think as long as we go out there on that field and give it everything we got and don't leave anything in the bag, we can look at ourselves with pride and be satisfied with what we have accomplished," Padres' pitcher Kevin Brown, a fierce opponent who would give the Yankees some tough moments, told the *Post*'s George King. "If it winds up that the breaks go our way and we win this whole thing, then so be it."

Yankee Stadium in October is like no other place on earth. The competitive spirit and camaraderie of the busiest, most ambitious city in the world converges on that 75-year old stadium with such force that the air seems to crackle with it. Every play is greeted with some kind of roar: grumbling when the enemy scores a base hit (by this point things have gone far beyond referring to the visiting team as "the visiting team"); horror when they score; a thunderclap of booing when a Yankee goofs, since even idols must be put in their place now and then; and jubilation at a Yankee run. A grand-slam homer from a Yankee bat triggers a roar that can cross county lines. New York fans live and die during their games and, when the World Series comes around, they become stronger and more powerful and relentless with each game won or lost. When the Yankees are winning, the atmosphere in and around the stadium is exhilarating; when they're losing, the collective frustration feels downright menacing.

Derek has a good understanding of the mixture of sports excellence and showmanship a good World Series demands. Playing a Series at Yankee Stadium, he told reporters the day before Game 1 versus the Padres, is "like a Broadway play, it's center stage. The World Series should be played in New York. Hopefully, it will be played here for a while. It's fun, it's the pinnacle of sports. The World Series is played in other cities, but it's never better than in New York.''

"I would imagine with the way New York gets about prime events," predicted David Cone, "it should be another frenzy."

Game 1 of the four-game sweep took place on a beautiful night in an atmosphere of high drama. The air shivered with sounds of anxiety in the early innings, when the Yanks were trailing and quailing under the formidable pitching skills of Padre Kevin Brown (whose undeniable talents provoked instant hatred in the spectators, in no mood for recognizing fine achievements made by the *other* team). Then, as Brown tired and was replaced and the Yankees boomed some incredible runs in the seventh inning (including a grand slam from Tino Martinez), like a whiplash, the mood reversed itself. Outside the stadium, the drumming of tens of thousands of impatient feet sounded like the initial rumbles of an earthquake ready to level the Bronx. Inside the intensity was even stronger and, as it became clear the Yankees were going to win Game 1, tension gave way to jubilation. The game won, 9-6, the departing Yanks were cheered by hundreds of fans who didn't mind staying way past midnight to salute them. As soon as the players were gone and people began heading home, you could feel the anxiety kicking in afresh: What about Game 2?

How does a young man like Derek Jeter handle such pressure? We've already discussed some of the sources of his strength: love of the game, belief in himself and his teammates, the support of his family. There's another one: religious faith. A Roman Catholic, Derek is one of several Yankees ministered to by Father Edward J. McMahon, a Jesuit priest who has been given the special assignment of ministering to the Catholic Yankees (of which there are, in fact, a number).

Before Game 2 of the Series, Father McMahon shared with Ursula Reel of the *Post* the subject of his most recent sermon: "The place of mercy in today's society." In a church often criticized for ignoring the differences between life inside it versus life outside, the celebrant (standing next to his assistant, Father Tom Prout) made it clear he knew baseball very well: "There is no mercy for anyone out on that field. The only Padres you should be feeling sorry for are the two standing in front of you." Despite the shock of umpires attending the service ("Father, how can you *say* that?") the team cheered and then pulverized the Padres with great skill, much passion, and no mercy.

Between prayers, McMahon, a seasoned Yankee-watcher, had a good eye for what made Derek so special a player. "He is a scientific batsman," he explained. He and [Paul] O'Neill and [Tino] Martinez sit in front of the TV for hours examining their swings. Then he goes down to that batting cage and *studies* his swing. Derek's like an old-timer; he goes after improvement so thoroughly, looking at everything. And he enjoys baseball: even in the worst times, when we're losing a game and the count is 0-2 in the bottom of the ninth and he's up, you look in his eyes and he's just having a ball! You know, I didn't expect to find that [kind of feeling] in the majors."

Humor is another way Derek keeps the tension from crippling his game. The same quick, daring wit Jeter demonstrated the night he poured a bottle of champagne on the forbidden head of George Steinbrenner is also noticeable between games and practice sessions. He will tease or banter with other players, or rough house. (The *Daily News* printed a photo of Derek putting fellow Yankee Tim Raines into a headlock.) He is said to be friendly with all his colleagues, including senior ones like Cone and Strawberry and O'Neill, but also good at not stepping on anybody's toes. Father McMahon says Derek is "liked by *everybody*—the batboys, the cafeteria women, the guards, the field people."

This Series is already being called anticlimactic by some, but it didn't feel that way when it was happening. A formidable team, the Padres didn't win a single game, but they didn't surrender easily, and their opponents never became overconfident. Each game was a battle from first confrontation at home plate to last.

In Game 2, Orlando Hernandez pitched seven utterly unflappable innings, as if his team's future World Series title was little cause for concern. And again, the hits kept coming, too much for the formidable Padres, who gave it up to the Bombers, 9-3.

Game 3, played in San Diego, was not so assured. It has been called one of the most nailbiting comebacks in memory. Once again, it was the seventh inning, and the Yanks were losing. And once again, they rallied, Scott Brosius zooming a run into the leftfield bleachers, followed by a double by Shane Spencer. Next inning, O'Neill and Martinez demonstrated another Yankee talent—walking. And then Brosius was back, hitting a perfect homer dead center. Back in their hometown, New Yorkers watched in awe, and noticed similar expressions on Padre fans. Although this game was not over, and there would be (at least) one more match to be fought, something told a lot of viewers that this Fall Classic was already wrapped up.

"We want to win," Derek told the *New York Times* the day before Game 4. "We never want to go into a situation where we think we can win one of two. We'll treat tomorrow like it's Game 7."

Bearing out that suspicion, Game 4 was a somewhat less torturous affair. Six innings in, after Bernie Williams drilled another power hit, Derek ran home to score the first Yankee run of the game. Derek dashed home again on a Brosius hit so powerful it broke his bat. Andy Pettitte pitched a heroic game (in a situation Torre must have found familiar, Pettitte's father was recovering from heart surgery), yielding in the eighth to Rivera— neither pitcher allowing a single run, the final score 3-0. And then it was really done. 125 wins, 50 losses. A nearly unbelievable season now had to be—it was history.

"This is the type of thing you dream about as a kid," Series MVP Scott Brosius, coming into his own as a champion hitter, admitted. Once again, the Yankees swarmed onto the ball field, collapsing in a huge pile of victory. Even the San Diegans gave them a standing ovation when it was all over. In the luster of the final triumph, celebrants naturally tried to place this amazing team in perspective: the best in a long time, the best for now, the best *period*?

"To me, this would be [the best team], because I'm part of this team and I'm very proud of what we accomplished this year," Bernie Williams told *News* writer Peter Botte. "When I look back at it, 10 or 15 years from now, I'm going to say I played with probably one of the best teams that ever played in the American League."

Looser from triumph and champagne, Derek hailed his team's achievement to the *Post*'s George King. "I don't see how you can say we aren't the greatest team ever. We are unselfish and we don't care who the hero is." This was another moment of completion for him: There could be no more doubts about his skills or his importance as a Yankee. He was no longer a rookie, but a crucial player for the greatest baseball team in the world.

By the middle of the night after that win, although Times Square was dotted with groups of cheering fans, the city was happy but mostly calm, having expected triumph and gotten it. (Besides, their energy had to be saved for the victory parade two days hence.) New Yorkers were stunned not only by the sight of their team winning, but of its owner, the unofficial municipal ogre, weeping with happiness. For once Steinbrenner seemed completely satisfied, thanking his players and manager and remembering Darryl Strawberry.

Well, not everyone was stunned. "It was actually good for Steinbrenner to have a good cry like that after the Yankees won the Series, because now he knows how so many of his secretaries have felt over the last 25 years," wrote Mike Lupica (who else?); he added for good measure, "Not to mention pitching coaches." That's New York.

Even in this moment of absolute triumph, somebody had to conjure up a little discord. That was done in a full-page article in the *New York Post* on October 21, 1998: "FEMALE FANS: DEREK YOU'VE STRUCK OUT."

"Derek Jeter is history," began the piece, written by Jeane MacIntosh and Libby Callaway, claiming that New York women "have lost their lust for the studly shortstop." It claimed the athlete himself comes across as "a cocky, club-hopping playboy—and out of league with the average woman." The piece went on to actually locate three women who had critical things to say about Jeter. One read Jeter's swagger at a recent party in his honor disapprovingly: "He could have had any woman there. And he walked around like he knew it."

A "former fan" chastised Jeter not only for having a relationship with Mariah Carey, but for ending it, deriding him for desiring "a spandex-wearing sexpot"— the kind of woman few Derek fans are. "It shatters illusions of him."

Right after bemoaning Jeter's lack of "substance," the *Post* story disclosed its own: "Every woman's fantasy is a guy with Derek Jeter's butt, but with the heart of a family man," a former Jeterette complained. "A woman is attracted to someone sexy and successful, but she also wants to be treated like a princess and have a family.''

The piece concluded with a subheadline, ''Pick out your favorite Yankee stud,'' picturing five other possible Yankee heartthrobs: Bernie Williams, Tino Martinez, Andy Pettitte, Paul O'Neill, and Shane Spencer (the only unmarried male of the bunch).

Two of the more mortifying journalistic bloopers are getting it wrong, and bad timing. This story appeared the very day the Yanks swept the World Series. Exactly 48 hours later, lower Manhattan was under siege from an onslaught of more than one million Yankee fans, come to celebrate their team's victory in a manner only New Yorkers can do, and do well: a ticker-tape parade commencing on Wall Street in lower Manhattan, turning onto Broadway and marching through the city's more than 200-year-old financial district to City Hall, where thousands of guests were waiting for a public ceremony. Of the million plus parade watchers, about 60 percent were female, ranging in age from six months to 72. Of those females, a diligent reporter could not find a single one with a remotely negative, critical, or dismissive opinion about the Yankees' shortstop. (The six-month-old, looking baffled and cranky [wet diaper], had no opinion.)

''Some women are just jealous,'' an older Jeter fan declared. ''They can't enjoy admiring Derek from afar, so they try to tear him down. And anyway, who wants to argue on a nice day like this?''

A younger admirer agreed, scorning the *Post* article and expressing relief that Jeter was once again ''up for grabs.'' She then was joined by several friends, all (like her) skipping high school that morning, and commenced screaming ''DEREK! I want you! DEERRREEEKKK . . . !''

(Mariah Carey apparently did not share these fans' opinions of the *Post* article. Almost a week later, the *Post*'s Richard Johnson reported the singer's distress over the story. She apparently didn't object to its claiming Jeter dumped her, or the negative picture it painted of her former beau [if Carey took issue with either, Johnson refrained from printing her comments]. No, what bugged Mariah was the story's description of her as a "spandex-wearing sexpot." "I don't wear spandex!" she objected. "What the hell is with you people? I haven't worn spandex since 1991. . . . Unless I'm on a treadmill, I'm not donning spandex.")

Anyway, it's true that Friday, October 23, was not a day for quarreling over tabloid news stories. There is nothing like victory to bring a city together under any circumstances. But *this* kind of hard and well-fought ensemble effort wrought by the 1998 New York Yankees was impossible to meet with anything but laughter and cheers. An hour before the parade began, papers thrown from Wall Street and Broadway windows were already clogging the parade route so seriously sanitation trucks began removing them. Traditionally, ticker tape (long, narrow printouts of the day's stock transactions) is the substance thrown on the honored marchers. In today's computer-driven world, ticker tape has become archaic, so from the windows came shredded memos, bills, old records, and, perhaps most of all, toilet paper, which does float gracefully, in long, sinuous lines, rather like the ticker tape of old.

On the sidewalks, the million-plus fans waved signs, bounced up and down, behaved with amazing cooperation, and cheered their lungs out. They sang and danced to music blasting from portable stereos. Everyone seemed to be playing the same songs, Queen's "We Are the Champions" and, by far the favorite, Tina Turner's "Simply the Best." Although schools and parents had issued stern warnings, there was an estimated 13 percent absentee rate in the city's school systems that morning, and a glance at the throngs in lower Manhattan answered the question of where all the missing students were. But who could really blame them? "Sometimes baseball can teach you more about life than a day in class," Mayor Giuliani, who allowed his own children to attend the parade, said. A few commentators accused the mayor of encouraging truancy, but Hizzoner wisely stayed out of the fight. The kids were having too great a time to care.

On several of the Yankees' floats, the players looked thrilled and also relieved. At first they waved back to the fans, whooping and smiling, but they also seemed to need to keep a distance between themselves and the crowd admiring them. Although the day was not overly sunny, many Yankees wore dark glasses, Derek included. (This caused momentary dismay among some Jeterettes: "Off with the glasses!" a few chanted as he passed.) If you looked closer, you noticed some Yankees appeared on the verge of tears, one or two letting go when the adulation became too much.

Maybe they couldn't help remembering how quickly even absolute triumph vanishes into thin air. A year from now, who knew if they would be in this perfect place again, or close to it, or even Yankees at all? Who knew if these same fans would be as thankful and happy, or would a tough season stir them to disapproval? (Even the optimistic Jeter knows how quickly the winds can change. James Kaplan reported an incident in his *New York* magazine profile: a fan asked Jeter to sign two baseballs, and then said "Thanks, man. Have a great year," as he left. Jeter turned to the reporter and responded "He'll be booin' me if I go oh-for-two, right?")

What would have been an emotional day for the team was made more so when they had gathered at Yankee

Stadium early that morning to be transported in buses to Wall Street for the parade; for there waiting for them, slightly weak and thin from his ordeal, but brandishing a big smile nonetheless, was Darryl Strawberry.

"Hey, Dog!" Derek cried delightedly, hugging the man many of his teammates had not seen since he went in for colon cancer surgery during the American League Division series. "It's great to see you. We missed you, man."

Convalescing during the Series, Strawberry would head the parade that morning, riding in a convertible with his wife, Charisse. As each wave of paradegoers realized who led the march, an emotional gasp was followed by waves of tears, blown kisses, even blessings to a clearly moved Strawberry. Careful not to overtax himself, he skipped the City Hall ceremony afterward, which became a long attempt to say thank you one more time.

Many lined downtown not only to salute their winning team, but to show devotion to one of its members. Signs of this tribute were everywhere: JETER IS SWEETER read one, held by a junior-high student who admitted she *and* her homeroom teacher were "Derek fanatics." DEREK DEREK DEREK! was another. YOU TRIED THE BLONDE, YOU DUSTED MARIAH, NOW SWEEP ME OFF MY FEET read still another. A small sign, prettily lettered and discreetly adorned by the player's team number, was simple and eloquent: I'M AVAILABLE.

Everywhere you looked, number twos were visible. On street corners, hawkers were running out of Jeter Yankee t-shirts, and almost called for help when fans began fighting over the last ones. Printed photos of Jeter swinging the bat heroically, or smiling into the camera irresistibly, sold like crazy, too. Unauthorized Jeter shirts, displaying pictures and even statistics, were popular favorites. In fact, by noon that day, Church Street, from the World Trade Center practically up to Canal Street, turned into an impromptu Jeter minimall, anything bearing his name or likeness changing hands instantly. ("All I got left is Hideki shirts," one salesman said plaintively; "We want *Derek*," a ring of frustrated customers bellowed.) This was nothing compared to what a little imagination and a lot of makeup could do: hundreds, no, *thousands* of Jeter fans simply painted their idol's name, or playing number, on their cheeks or foreheads (one very skillful young lady squeezed a "DJ" onto her nose!), trying not to disturb their work at least until the subject of their admiration drove by and admired it.

When the loved one appeared to them, on the second Yankee float, the volume level in downtown, already deafening, grew almost lethal, the action behind the barricades went frenzied. Although the player himself seemed genial and low key, in brown sports clothes and dark shades, his hair grown a bit longer, ballistic admiration followed him every inch of the parade. If anyone had ever wondered if Jetermania was just some publicist's scam, two minutes on lower Broadway that day would have corrected their misperception. "Your city," several fans chanted as they waved to Derek passing by, "*Your city!*" sounding like they were saluting a prince, not a baseball player.

"Every team from now on that has a good season is going to be compared to the 1998 Yankees. And, I predict that, when the history of this game is finally written, it will be the greatest team of all time," the Mayor intoned, back at City Hall Park.

Torre was gracious: "These guys are the best who have ever played baseball."

Player after player gave thanks. The crowd began chanting for their favorites: "Bernie, Bernie" they would begin, and Bernie Williams rose to speak. After the World Series trophy had been displayed to volleys of "Ooooooh"'s, after Tony Bennett sang "America the Beautiful" as he had before Game 1 of the Series, and after many speeches were politely or feverishly applauded, the emcees could no longer hold back the New York Yankee the crowd called for all day: they awarded the first honorary key to New York City to Derek Jeter, and amid gigantic noises of approval their favorite, stepping to the podium, looking all the more dashing, briefly spoke his thanks.

"I don't think there's a person in the world who's been more spoiled than I've been," he began (immediately interrupted by screams and applause). "I've had an opportunity to win two world championships in my first three years. I'm playing in the best city, for the best owner, the best manager, and in front of the best fans in the world." (More screams, more applause.) "There's only one thing that went wrong with this season in my opinion, and that is, we didn't get an opportunity to win the World Series at home. I guess we're gonna have to come back and do it next year." (Huge screams, huge applause as he takes his key to the city and waves, sitting down on a stage full of Yankees beaming agreement.)

Yeah—it's his city, all right.

Pride of the Yankees

"A life is not important, except in the impact it has on other lives."

—Jackie Robinson

"How cool is it to be Derek Jeter?" asked the *New York Post*'s Anthony L. Gargano. The *News*'s Peter Botte went further: "Is there anybody you'd rather be in New York than Derek Jeter?" Nobody scoffed at the rhapsodies. Veteran TV news reporter Penny Crone, used to journalistic combat—chasing mobsters and politicians for quotes, filing spunky live reports—stood outside Yankee Stadium after Game 2 of the 1998 World Series looking flabbergasted amid triumphant Jeter fanatics who had painted his name, his team number, little hearts, and messages of affection all over their faces.

Jeter's achievement and popularity amaze and thrill observers near and far. Father McMahon, Yankee priest, has said "Every now and then [Derek] says 'I've been terribly spoiled.' He knows that God has been good to him. He's very serious about his religion. 'Things have been going too good for me.' But he doesn't worry about that—this kid is the type that could absorb a lot more gifts from God. Some people, when they become powerful or famous, get a little out of touch. Derek will never be that way."

"He's worked. He's worked hard. He's sharing his gifts with all of us, and I think that's the greatest thing

anyone can do," says his former teacher, Shirley Garzelloni. "The one thing I used to wonder about Derek
was if he ever realized how intelligent he was. I guess
in baseball it's the same way: he never thought about
being anything less than the best. And I don't mean that
in the sense he came off as aggressive or pompous:
There was just a natural flow of effort. There were certain expectations, and he just *met* the expectations of
his parents, his friends, the community, the teams he
played on."

He is part of a team that not only reasserts baseball
as a sport about not single stars but collective effort—
let's call it The Torre Doctrine—but embodies a
broader face for that sport. It was not until 1947 that
Jackie Robinson, joining the Brooklyn Dodgers and becoming that season's Rookie of the Year, forged a decisive crack in the color barrier that baseball had
shamefully but doggedly enforced throughout its history. Two generations later, a young man whose very
identity challenges that barrier by coming from both
sides of it is one of the game's most beloved figures.
When Derek Jeter attended a sports writers' dinner recently to receive an award, he was preceded at the podium by Robinson's widow. He began his own speech
"I just want to say that one of the main rewards of
winning this award is the opportunity to sit up here next
to a woman like Mrs. Robinson." Reading that statement, you feel an enormous bond forming between, and
holding, the athletes of the past (problems and all) and
those of the present and future.

Roger Jackson is a New York City writer and researcher; his daughter Allison is not only a Jeter fan but
shares Jeter's racial background—Jackson is African-
American, his former wife German-Irish. Watching Je-

ter's career and popularity with young people has given him a lot to think about.

"In the society we live in today there are so many things, like money and race, that separate us from each other. Being a biracial young man sets [Jeter] apart further. But through hard work and belief in himself, he's made something extraordinary of his life—and kids are drawn to that."

It's been noted that among the swarms of young fans waiting for Jeter before and after games, many are like him: from more than one, sometimes several, races and ethnicities. With each generation, as Americans slowly relinquish the polarizations that blight our history, greater numbers of such children appear, often rejected or ignored by others. Such kids reach out to Derek not only because they admire his achievement but recognize in it, his all-accepting public manner, and his public's enthusiasm for him, something of their own hoped-for futures.

Allison Jackson, her father remembers, "didn't know Derek was biracial. What I try and do is, whenever somebody like that comes along, I'll say to Allison 'He's like you.' " Unknowingly, Jackson echoes Mariah Carey's remark, "I had never met anybody like that, and that's always been a big part of who I am." Allison, her father says, is "beginning to see that there are not only other people like her but that they're not maladjusted or tagged with the label stuck on kids of interracial marriages, 'What about the children?' The children we now know turn into Halle Berry, Mariah Carey, Derek Jeter, and other valuable Americans."

There's something encouraging about such a person being idolized by a public that often still doesn't know how to get along with itself. (This is not to suggest an ending of racism: about that, Jackson tersely adds, "We need to grow up about issues of race. We have to stop playing *Gone With the Wind* or *Soul on Ice*.'') Jackson continues, ''Jeter isn't Mickey Mantle. Mantle represented a different age: the blonde, blue-eyed ideal. Just about the only people that don't seem to be looked on as flawed in America are 'blonde-blues'—the only people who can escape criticism. But Derek represents the kid who is the contemporary popular figure to young people—he's cool, he's really good looking, he's nice. Any parent would like to see a young man like that walk through the door. That's why when I see girls in the neighborhood, or in the stands at Yankee Stadium, wearing Jeter hats and jerseys, they're all persuasions. And that's important.''

Now, of course, millions of people have many kinds of expectations of Derek Jeter. He's already made the grade; what lies ahead? Plenty.

Paul Morgan, a longtime observer of the sport and Derek, has high hopes. ''I expect him to continue to have seasons like he's had. He's handled the New York style well; he's got a firm ground now in New York, a home in Tampa, specifically bought it to be as close to training as possible. I don't know if he would ever get to [a batting average of] .400, but remember, he's only 24.''

In the wake of the Yankees' World Series sweep, hopes for Jeter's future were sent aloft from all sides. Within minutes of their final win, NY 1's sportscasters Budd Mishkin and Steve Cangiolosi were discussing the player's future with an organization that would spend the autumn in grueling contract negotiations to forge a new team for 1999—and that season's World Series run. Mishkin expressed the hopes of many when he wished the Yankees would keep Jeter in New York for the next decade. Within days, articles and commentary public and private suggested a ''career contract,'' ensuring Jeter remaining with the team that inspired and then benefited from him.

"Career-length contract? I could see him doing that easily," says Morgan. "His marriage with New York is terrific. He grew up as a Yankee fan. He's having the time of his life."

And longtime speculation gathered steam on another topic—that Jeter's model behavior on and off the field would lead to his becoming the Yankees' captain. There hasn't been one since Don Mattingly, a player as revered as Jeter, left the team just as Derek was joining it. Derek would be only the eleventh captain in Yankee history, following Mattingly and Hal Chase (in 1912), Roger Peckinpaugh (1914–21), Babe Ruth (but for only six games, in 1922), Everett Scott (1922–25), Lou Gehrig (1935–41), Thurman Munson (1976–79; both Gehrig and Munson's reigns ended with their premature deaths), Graig Nettles (1982–84), Ron Guidry (1986–89), and Derek's coach, Willie Randolph (1986–88). Captain would be the crown on Jeter's efforts, but (perhaps shrewdly) he has kept this issue at a distance. Joe Torre, David Cone, and others inside and outside the Yankees have acknowledged the possibility. For now, there is really no need of a captain, with several fine leaders like Cone and Paul O'Neill and Bernie Williams completing their careers in pinstripes. In a few seasons, however, with who knows what kind of team emerging from the glow of the Yankees' first century (and whether or not they will stay in their beloved Bronx stadium), with Joe Torre and players and coaches inevitably moving on or retiring, Derek's leadership will finally be put to the test.

Is there anyone who has followed this guy's life that would guess him not to be up to the challenge? It is not, as yet, guaranteed he will stay a Yankee, but it seems hard to imagine even Steinbrenner (if he remains the

Boss) withstanding the fallout from letting Jeter walk away from the Bronx Bombers. Jeter is still some time from free-agent status. Even though one can't picture Derek and his agent coolly deciding to try their luck elsewhere, we simply can't predict what will happen. (A glimpse is provided by Jeter's behavior when negotiations for 1998 ran close to the wire—he made it clear that an unresolved contract wasn't going to keep him off the ballfield.)

Besides, Derek has always had more on his mind than baseball. With that unaffected willfulness he demonstrates in play, he has begun to capitalize on his fame in ways that have nothing to do with endorsements and arbitration. He's using fame to help others.

Jeter knows his star power can impact the public in ways beyond sheer celebrity. He was taught, early, about responsibility and actions not only for oneself, but for others. "Doing something for the community" is the kind of responsible phrase some today might find old-fashioned; the Jeters understand how essential such a concept, and the responsibility underlying it, is to a person's well-being, and that of the society he or she lives in.

So, it should not have been surprising in 1996, amid World Series celebrations, when Derek Jeter established the Turn 2 Foundation. (The number in the title rather than the word *to* is a play on his own team number. "One good turn deserves another," is one of the group's slogans.)

Turn 2 is what's known in the not-for-profit world as a "nonoperational foundation": It raises money not for its own building or programs, but to support other organizations conducting work it deems worthwhile. The foundation's central concern is the prevention and treatment of teenage substance abuse-related problems. Programs Turn 2 supports include The Boys and Girls Club of New York and the Phoenix Academy. The foundation's efforts are not restricted to New York: The YMCA/Black Achiever Program in Western Michigan is another beneficiary of Turn 2's fundraising efforts.

It is also surprising to see Jeter hard at work at this cause, because often a personal misfortune impels a person into one branch of social work or another. The ranks of alcohol or drug-abuse counselors are full of people in recovery themselves. Jeter's intensely focused, disciplined life left him little opportunity for such problems. It was this precocious awareness of the importance of remaining committed to the great goal of his childhood and youth that carried Jeter so swiftly to success, and so adroitly through the turbulent, problem-prone years of adolescence. It's this unique experience he also has to share with the young people eager to listen to him because of that effort's results.

"The latest news from the U.S. Department of Health and Human Services," he writes in the foundation Spring 1998 newsletter, *The Turn 2 Spirit*, "is very disturbing regarding the teen use of alcohol and drugs. The report states the perceived risk of using alcohol, marijuana and cocaine among teens has decreased from 1994 to 1996. In addition, more than 18 percent of children ages 12 to 17 are using alcohol, and the use of marijuana remains the most widely used drug among adolescents."

So, Jeter's concerns seem motivated not by personal redemption but simple caring: "Kids need positive influence in their lives and I hope to guide them in the right direction." It's taking on a lot for a young man still developing his own career in one of the most competitive fields in the world to also be responsible for raising money to help troubled kids survive the obstacles with which fate or misfortune have burdened them. Not only must Jeter commit himself to raising funds from personal and private sources, he has pledged a chunk of his own earnings to the foundation as well. He even managed to turn his commercial endorsements into fund-raising opportunities: "Some people wondered why I decided to sign with Fila as opposed to another company," he explained. "But this company was interested in helping my off-the-field cause."

At a ceremony to launch another wing of his social action efforts, "Jeter's Leaders," a group that recognizes outstanding teenagers in the New York area, Derek's dad reiterated "The emphasis is on Derek's off-the-field focus—a worthwhile cause of helping young people and giving something back to his community."

Faced with the desire to give back to the community and the daunting challenges of this effort, when the question arose of who would handle the daily running of Turn 2, Derek turned to someone in whom he had unquestioning confidence—his father. Dr. Charles Jeter had a full-time practice back in Kalamazoo, focusing on patients with substance abuse and psychiatric problems. At 49, it couldn't have been a casual gesture to put aside his own career, but he heeded his son's call for help, and became Turn 2's executive director and vice president. Derek's mother, Dorothy, and sister, Sharlee, currently attending college in Georgia, share secretary/treasurer duties.

"I'm impacting more people this way than I was in private practice," Dr. Jeter told Jack Curry of the *New York Times*. "It wasn't a hard decision. I saw this as a chance to work with Derek beyond the father-son relationship."

How far beyond that relationship this not-for-profit partnership went was immediately noted by Curry, who quoted Jeter "sound[ing] like George Steinbrenner" and telling the *Times* reporter, "I'm still the boss. I tell him [Dr. Jeter] what to do."

In a curious way, the younger Jeter's taking on social work is another mirroring of the life and decisions made by the elder. Dr. Jeter attended Fisk University and played shortstop for their baseball team; Derek Jeter, of course, not only focused on baseball but the same position. Dr. Jeter didn't pursue sports professionally, but turned to psychotherapy and social work; Derek, in the midst of one of the most successful baseball careers in modern times, now enlarges his public scope assisting his dad's own profession. It's another illustration of the extraordinary parallels and coordinations in this very close, committed family.

In February 1997 nearly 600 people attended a kick-off fundraising dinner for the foundation at the Radisson Plaza at Kalamazoo Center. Both private and corporate donors presented checks or participated in silent and live auctions of baseball memorabilia and autographed items. Turn 2's father and son team were clearly delighted by the turnout and generosity demonstrated that night.

"The support for the foundation is just great," Derek commented. "I wanted to give back to the community and this is a great way to do it."

"Look at the support for this," Dr. Jeter enthused. The hall was full of not only adult fund-raisers but smiling children, whose seats were sponsored by local companies. The event's success was not simply a validation of Derek Jeter's new star power, but a tribute to what he was planning to do with it. The Jeters and their supporters also know how to exploit Derek's popularity without appearing unseemly: An occasion like Derek's birthday is turned into a party that is also a fund-raiser (a recent event was held, appropriately, at New York's All-Star Café). On June 26, 1997, Jeter celebrated his birthday in SoHo, where a huge mural of the player painted on the side of a building was unveiled. The mural, commissioned by Fila, became a tourist site for Derek's fans: Almost every day, some could be seen having their pictures taken beneath it.

A second fundraising dinner was held back in Kalamazoo on January 10, 1998.* And some of the foundation's events were simple treats for kids in need of them. Seventy students from the Kalamazoo Area Academic Achievement Group were taken to Detroit to see Jeter play in Tiger Stadium. The guests had a session with Derek before the game, in which he spoke encouragingly about staying in school (K.A.A.A.P. targets academically at-risk students). Turn 2 also hosted more than 300 young Kalamazooans and their parents at an International Hockey League game at Wings Stadium in which Jeter dropped the ceremonial opening puck.

All these efforts, and the other elements mentioned in this chapter—the continuing high standard of performance in baseball, the possibility of being Yankee captain, the caring beyond the field—flows into its title, also the title of this book: *Pride of the Yankees*. This is not a lightly given label, as anyone familiar with baseball knows. It has been used in connection with Derek by other writers and sports lovers. It was given almost three quarters of a century ago to one of the very greatest Yankees, first baseman Lou Gehrig. The son of German working-class immigrants living on Manhattan's Upper East Side (now a much more exclusive neighborhood where many of the city's elite—including Derek Jeter—live), Henry Louis Gehrig was born in 1903. His early life was very unlike Jeter's: poor and uncertain, physically unpromising, he created, through sheer will, an extraordinary athletic and academic career that brought him to Columbia University and, eventually, farther north to brand-new Yankee Stadium. He had an extraor-

---

*Donations or inquiries may be sent to: Turn 2 Foundation, Inc., P.O. Box 19158, Kalamazoo MI 49019, (616) 349-0818.

dinary baseball life, his unbroken presence on the Yankees' starting lineup beginning on June 1, 1925, and ending with Gehrig's 2,130th game on April 30, 1939. It took more than half a century for another player, Baltimore's Cal Ripken, Jr., to break that record.

Gehrig's example and destiny cast a long shadow over baseball. What took him out of the lineup, finally, wasn't maturity, but the illness that eventually killed him, a degenerative motor disorder then called *amyotrophic lateral sclerosis*—now, more simply, ALS or Lou Gehrig's Disease. The impact Gehrig's tragedy had on the entire country, then emerging from the Great Depression and bracing itself for the Second World War, cannot be underestimated. The prospect of this powerful, gifted man wasting away in his thirties was too much for many to accept, or understand. Not long after voluntarily benching himself, the Yankees honored Gehrig; at that ceremony, on July 4, 1939, the Pride of the Yankees made the greatest speech in a sport not known for its speeches.

"Fans," he began, "for the past two weeks you have been reading about the bad break I got. Yet today I consider myself the luckiest man on the face of the earth. I have been in ballparks for 17 years and have never received anything but kindness and encouragement from you fans." He thanked his teammates, current and former; that day, Gehrig's long-standing troubled relationship with former teammate Babe Ruth was settled when Ruth wept in Gehrig's arms. He thanked his Yankee manager, who had refused to bench him even when his health began to fail. He thanked the Stadium groundskeepers. He thanked his parents, his wife, even his mother-in-law. "I close in saying that I may have had a tough break, but I have an awful lot to live for." Then he was finished.

This moment defined integrity for a generation of

Americans. The great ballplayer was revealed once and for all as a great man. For those who love the sport, it still has tremendous power, in part because baseball's greatest movie, a biography of Gehrig released in 1942, a year after the player's death at 37, reenacts it. At the end of *The Pride of the Yankees*, Gehrig (played by Gary Cooper) ends his speech of farewell. The words echo in the still Yankee air. He turns and walks past his players, his wife (Teresa Wright), enters the empty dugout, and walks off into its shadows. This is the favorite movie of pretty much every baseball fan. It is said to be a favorite of Derek Jeter's.

Why do people connect him with Gehrig? Certainly not because of the end of the story. Another great Yankee, Jim "Catfish" Hunter, was recently diagnosed with Lou Gehrig's Disease, and no one would dream of wishing a similar fate on Derek Jeter. No, it's that sense that there is more than a great shortstop out there—that everything we've noted over the course of this book suggests, as well, the possibility of a great man. There are never enough of these, especially in public life, and when we sense a real one, we don't just applaud the guy—we rally to him.

A recent expression of this belief comes from a *GQ* profile by Peter Richmond. In the face of through-the-roof salary packages, rampant commercialization of the sport, and even Yankee Stadium itself suddenly considered disposable by George Steinbrenner, Richmond admits discouragement, until he thinks of Jeter and his integrity: "I knew he'd been summoned by the baseball gods: to carry the torch, to help save the team and the Stadium and maybe even the game of baseball itself."

This sense of Derek as someone precious, almost a healer of the sport, has existed throughout his short career. At the end of the 1996 season, Kalamazoo's Jack Moss sounded the same note when he wrote, "Derek

Jeter is everything right in a world of sports that is often wrong.'' Moss praised him as ''the epitome of the American dream,'' ''a young man who is intelligent, personable, caring and, well, everything that is good about young people. He is the ultimate role model for countless youngsters, not only here but around the country. Perhaps around the world.

''If it seems that we, among many, have placed Jeter on a pedestal, it is because he is most deserving of that status.''

Another great man, Mario Cuomo, even found something instructive in the publicity blitz surrounding Derek's dating Mariah Carey. ''There's something refreshing about someone who could go out in a limousine with Mariah Carey and yet not make an ass of himself. His ability to handle all that is inspiring—you can do a lot of things in life without losing your class, your dignity.''

It's Jeter's life in baseball that is the keystone to all this, of course, and the former Governor of New York concluded talking about Jeter by saying, ''I hope he plays for the Yankees for a long, long time.''

Paul Morgan likes the Pride of the Yankees title, too. ''He just epitomizes what's good with baseball in general: a hardworking kid playing, having a good time. You're seeing more of that in baseball again—you see it in McGwire, Sosa, A-Rod. But Derek, for loving and knowing the game, holding it special and honoring it, is at the very top.''

He pauses a second, realizing he's been speaking for a long time and still has more to say about this player he's followed through his whole career. Almost apologetically, he concludes, ''It's real easy to talk about Derek.''

But if it's easy to venerate a person, it must be hard to be alone on that pedestal. What will come next? Well, the pursuit of that perfect game, the error-free, 1.000 baseball record. Mario Cuomo, when that ambition of Derek's was repeated to him, responded ''Well. He understands perfection. That's interesting.''

In baseball, anything can happen. Getting his foot caught in the outfield and injuring himself during a run for a catch altered (some would say destroyed) Mickey Mantle's life, leading to the catastrophic injuries and health problems that felled one of the most magnificent of all baseball talents. Every time Jeter takes one of those kamikaze flights through the air to get the ball, a part of us gulps in worry. The concern is tempered by the sureness of remembering he is an athlete, a great one, and knows in most situations out there how to take care of himself. That he has been relegated to the disabled list only once so far is a sign he may stay off it for much of his career.

Baseball remains his home, the place he can most be himself, and even though that home dwells in an open stadium before tens of thousands of people, and the stadiums morph from one city to another, it's still, in every sense, *his* home, the way it was once Ruth's, and Mantle's, and Robinson's.

We can wish him a long and productive life in which the sport he cares for never lets him down. The image of his great Yankee predecessor Joe DiMaggio in his hospital bed at 83, fighting life-threatening pneumonia, yet insisting on watching his team win the 1998 World Series on TV, still knowing his sport so well he can predict the plays and pitches ahead of time, is a haunting one, but also comforting.

Once you're in the game, you never really leave it.

Some people find what they love and are good at it and make it their lives. We are fascinated by such unique, powerful, fortunate examples. Maybe we look at them too much for their own comfort, but we can't help looking.

Much of Derek's life will nonetheless—and despite considerable scrutiny—remain private. No one could imagine Jeter on a daytime talk show, confessing his phobias or hawking personal misfortunes for publicity. It's just not the kind of thing he would do, since so much of him is firmly grounded in self-respect. (A fan hearing some of the more lurid rumors about Jeter's behavior during the Carey affair dismissed them with a headshake and "No. It's just not in character for him to act like that.") However, he will still be asked questions about Mariah Carey, and he will still sigh and roll his eyes over the whole thing. (The *Post*'s Gargano demanded, "Would you like to be asked 12 times a day about your ex?") He will probably get married someday, and the fans who see him at the altar will eventually get over it.

He remains a new kind of star: one who is as celebrated by baseball lovers as he is by the larger public. People who don't go to ball games know who Derek Jeter is, and admire him. And a generation of teenagers wish they could be him, or know him, or marry him (or, at least, date him). Jeter doesn't take that admiration lightly. When it gets too clamorous, it must seem a burden, but usually he is able to handle the acclaim and the attention with equal grace. He should become only better at both, with time.

A longtime baseball lover links Jeter's on-field and off-field behavior. "The crucial question about a shortstop is always, Can they make the play in the hole? Can they get to the popup to short left field, that no-man's-land that is a shortstop's territory? Jeter can make every play a shortstop has to make—and he can do everything *else* a ballplayer needs to do.

"And the media attention is another challenge, another ground ball deep in the hole. But this time [off the field], the play is emotional, interpersonal, sexual—and the media's watching. Even a great shortstop shouldn't be presupposed to have the guts to handle *this* play. But he does. Jeter dealt with all that attention (concerning himself and Carey) in a way that didn't make him look like an idiot. The press would have dogged him all year about this, over and over, if he hadn't handled it with such self-respect. Pretty amazing—like every other part of him.''

We know what this guy could be doing in the off-season: taking it easy, reaping the benefits of a heroic season by going coast-to-coast as The Baseball Star, appearing at shopping malls, sports cards conventions, sports stores openings, television (he has already appeared on *Seinfeld*) . . . living a life of public attention and promotional fees. Other players, in all the professional sports fields, make good on their hard work in this way.

Jeter, however, has already spelled out his plans for the near future: he'll spend the off-season preparing for next season.

The Yankees maintain a spring training complex in Tampa, Florida, the site of the start of Derek's professional baseball career—remember, that was less than *seven* years ago. Once the World Series and its celebrations are done, Jeter won't be doing any of the sports hero things. He has announced he will head down to Tampa, to spend the winter preparing for next season.

''You've got to keep things in perspective,'' he told Ken Davidoff, a staff writer for the *Bergen Record*. And then he added what could be taken for his own credo: ''Baseball comes first. That's your job. You have to do it. And everything else is second.''

The public's admiration is something Derek takes very well. He believes, however, that some of it is sheer sports mania. (''It's been a good year for baseball, I

think baseball is recognized more all over," he has said.)
When the depth of that admiration is revealed, he ac-
knowledges it, is awed by it, and even humbled.

After the 1996 World Series and New York's downtown revels, Jeter returned to Kalamazoo for another celebration. His hometown was as delirious in victory as
had been his newfound home. Almost 3,000 gathered in
Kalamazoo Central High School's gym to honor their
neighbor and friend. Jeter was welcomed by the school
principal, and he shared the applause with his proud parents. The program lasted over an hour, with musical tributes from the school marching band and introductions
from former teacher Sally Padley and former teacher and
varsity coach Don Jackson, who declared "We've
hosted Bill Clinton and Bob and Elizabeth Dole, but
nothing matches this."

Then, Jeter's sister Sharlee, a senior at Kalamazoo
Central, delivered remarks, as graceful a speaker as her
brother is a baseball player, in which she thanked Derek
for being "someone who has made me realize that hard
work does pay off," for being such a fine brother, and
"for giving me my own identity."

Jeter, according to the *Kalamazoo Gazette*'s report,
was very much moved. "When my parents told me that
Kalamazoo wanted to honor me, I figured 20 or 30 people would show up and most of them would be my old
coaches and teachers." He sounded like this afternoon
was an affirmation even beyond those that must have
accompanied his dream.

There were still more honors to come, from lines of
kids waiting for him to autograph their baseball cards,
ball mitts, anything to do with him and the game. It was
one of those special moments when many people ac-
knowledge one person has done something that means a
lot to them, and they stop to give gratitude.

You can page through baseball history books and find

remnants of such moments in them. In words and pictures spanning a century, generations urban and rural came together, played, celebrated not just winning but the game itself. Baseball meant not only visibility and victory and endorsements. It meant community, and achievement, and integrity. When people from all over look at Derek Jeter's picture, or watch him play, they see not just the handsome young man or the famous athlete. They recognize him as someone who embodies the values that sustain worthy effort. It is a sign of the sport's luck that, at its latest low point, when greed, suspicion, and cynicism threatened to make us forget what was so great about baseball in the first place, once again a young man who knew what the game *has* to be about burst into view, not only ensuring his own success but helping to rescue what he loves from abandonment.

Admirers covering themselves with number twos and carrying Jeter photographs like icons recognize this quality, too. "There are lots of handsome guys out there," one says outside Yankee Stadium after a game, "but Derek is much more than handsome. He's the kind of guy you'd be proud to know, and go out with—at least, I *hope* to be proud to go out with someday!" The dad of another teenager hopping with impatience for Jeter to appear adds "It's not easy to find public figures today you can point to and tell your kids 'That's the guy you should take after.' I'm glad Jeter does what he does, and doesn't brag about it. We need more like him. Our kids need a lot more like him."

"It's not just that he's a charming fellow," an older woman asserts, who when she saw Jeter pass by a minute later shouted words of love, forgetting she was standing right next to her own husband (too enthusiastic himself to care). "He has such character, such dedication, such," and she pounces on the next, perfect word, ''*guts*. Remember guts? Nice to see all that in a young man.''

Whatever he does in the future, a rapt world will have a great time watching.

Bibliography

Selected Books

Frommer, Harvey. *The New York Yankee Encyclopedia*. New York: Macmillan Publishing Company, 1997.

Goodwin, Doris Kearns. *Wait Till Next Year*. New York: Simon & Schuster, 1997.

Harper, John, and Bob Klapisch. *Champions!* New York: Villard Books, 1996.

King, George. *Unbeatable!* New York: HarperCollins Publishers, 1998.

Nickson, Chris. *Mariah Carey Revisited*. New York: St. Martin's Press, 1998.

Pepe, Phil. *The Yankees*. Dallas: Taylor Publishing Company, 1995.

Ripken, Cal, Jr., and Mike Bryan. *The Only Way I Know*. New York: Viking Penguin, 1997.

Torre, Joe, and Tom Verducci. *Chasing the Dream*. New York: Bantam Books, Inc., 1997.

Ward, Geoffrey C., and Ken Burns. *Baseball*. New York: Random House, 1994.

Winfield, Dave, and Tom Parker. *Winfield: A Player's Life*. New York: Norton, 1988.

Selected Publications

Note: All facts and statements in this biography are derived from interviews conducted by the author in 1998 or from previously published material. Efforts to obtain a statement or verification of facts from Derek Jeter (through his agent at International Management Group) were unsuccessful. Previously published material consulted and cited includes the following publications and bylines:

Arizona Republic: Pedro Gomez

Bergen Record: Mark J. Czerwinski, Ken Davidoff, Rafael Hermoso, Bob Hertzel, Bob Klapisch, Tara Sullivan, Adrian Wojnarowski

Columbus Dispatch: Derek Monroe

ESPN/ESPN The Magazine: Dave Campbell, Dan Patrick

Gentleman's Quarterly (GQ): Devin Friedman, Peter Richmond

Hartford Courant: Jack Connell

In Style: Elysa Gardner

Interview: Veronica Webb

Kalamazoo Gazette: Mickey Ciokajlo, Paul Morgan, Jack Moss

New York: James Kaplan

New York Daily News: Peter Botte, D.L. Cummings, Luke Cyphers, Mitchell Fink, Mike Lupica, Joanna Molloy, George Rush, Larry Sutton

New York Post: Libby Callaway, Anthony L. Gargano, Jay Greenberg, Richard Johnson, Tom Keegan, Kevin Kernan, George King, Jeane MacIntosh, Ursula Reel, Joel Sherman, George Willis

New York Times: Dave Anderson, Jack Curry, Nick Friedman, Tom Friend, Buster Olney

Newsday: Mark Hermann, Shaun Powell, Kelly Whiteside

St. Louis Post-Dispatch: Mike Eisenbath

Sports Illustrated: Mark Bechtel, Tom Verducci, Kelly Whiteside

The Sporting News: Michael Knisley

Steppin' Out: Chauncé Hayden

USA Today: Bill Koenig

Vibe: Danyel Smith

Vogue: Vicki Woods

Yankees: Mark Balk, Joanna Cohen, Alan Schwarz

Derek Jeter at a Glance

Name: Derek Sanderson Jeter
Height: 6'3"
Weight: 185
Eyes: Green
Position: Shortstop
Team: New York Yankees
Player Number: 2
Bats: Right
Throws: Right
Birthday: June 26, 1974; Pequannock, New Jersey
Hometown: Kalamazoo, Michigan (moved there at age four)
Currently Resides: Tampa, Florida (in off-season); New York, New York (during season); Kalamazoo, Michigan (parents' residence)
Mailing Address: Derek Jeter
                     c/o New York Yankees
                     Yankee Stadium
                     161st Street and River Avenue
                     Bronx, New York 10451
Internet: http://www.yankees.com

Career Statistics

YEAR	CLUB	AVG	G	AB	R	H	2B	3B	HR	RBI	BB	SO	SB
1992	Tampa	.202	47	173	19	35	10	0	3	25	19	36	2
	Greensboro	.243	11	37	4	9	0	0	1	4	7	16	0
1993	Greensboro	.295	128	515	85	152	14	11	5	71	58	95	18
1994	Tampa (FSL)	.329	69	292	61	96	13	8	0	39	23	30	28
	Albany	.377	34	122	17	46	7	2	2	13	15	16	12
	Columbus	.349	35	126	25	44	7	1	3	16	20	15	0
1995	Columbus	.317	123	486	96	154	27	9	2	45	61	56	20
	Yankees	.250	15	48	5	12	4	1	0	7	3	11	0
1996	Yankees	.314	157	582	104	183	25	6	10	78	48	102	14
1997	Yankees	.291	159	654	116	190	31	7	10	70	74	125	23
1998	Yankees	.324	149	626	127	203	25	8	19	84	57	119	30
Totals:													
	Minor League	.306	447	1751	307	536	78	31	16	213	203	264	90
	Major League	.308	480	1910	352	588	85	22	39	239	182	357	67

AVG: Batting average; G: Number of games; AB: At Bats; R: Runs; H: Hits; 2B: Doubles; 3B: Triples; HR: Home Runs; RBI: Runs Batted In; BB: Walks; SO: Strike Outs; SB: Stolen Bases.

MORE WINNING SPORTS BOOKS
FROM ST. MARTIN'S PAPERBACKS

MARCUS:
The Autobiography of Marcus Allen,
with Carlton Stowers
From his triumphant rise to football stardom to his friendship with O.J. Simpson, get the real story—in his own
words—on Heisman Trophy winner Marcus Allen.

HANG TIME:
Days and Dreams with Michael Jordan,
by Bob Greene
Journalist and bestselling author Bob Greene follows sports
legend Michael Jordan for two seasons with the Chicago
Bulls, and uncovers some amazing things about the athlete—
and the man.

MICHAEL JORDAN, by Mitchell Krugel
A head-to-toe portrait of basketball's phenomenal Michael
Jordan—on and off the court, in intimate detail.

THIS GAME'S THE BEST!
So Why Don't They Quit Screwing With It?
by George Karl with Don Yaeger
The fiery, funny, outspoken head coach of the Seattle
Supersonics cuts loose on the sport of basketball and all its
players.

AVAILABLE WHEREVER BOOKS ARE SOLD
FROM ST. MARTIN'S PAPERBACKS